2026 HEMP BUILDING DIRECTORY

Guide to the International Hemp Building Industry

HEMP BUILDING DIRECTORY 2026

Cape Cod Hemp House, MA. Photo courtesy of C.H. Newton Builders

HEMP BUILDING DIRECTORY 2026
Guide to the International Hemp Building Industry

PUBLISHED BY HAEPENNY, LLC
COPYRIGHT ©2026 BY JEAN LOTUS

All rights reserved. Neither this book, nor any parts within it may be sold or reproduced in any form or by any electronic or other mechanical means, including information storage and retrieval systems without permission in writing from the publisher. The only exception is by a reviewer who may quote short excerpts in a review.

Cover and page design by Megann Fowler

The resources contained herein may not be continuously updated but provide a source of information to begin your search. Haepenny, LLC assumes no responsibility for the accuracy of claims of the companies and/or products listed, nor does the publisher guarantee or endorse the services, sales, or products themselves.

Printed in the United States of America
ISBN: 979-8-9854193-8-2

TABLE OF CONTENTS

Introduction 7

CHAPTER 1:
EDUCATION, ADVOCACY & TRAINING

• Article: CA Hempcrete ADU Build with French Panel Prototypes 10

• Leader Profile: James Kitchin, Bio-Based Materials Collective 12

• Leader Profile: Clifton "Ray" Kaderli, Hemp Build Network 13

• Listings: Education, Advocacy & Training 14

• Leader Profile: Lisa Sundberg, Indigenous Habitat Institute 20

• Leader Profile: Kristin Orr-Santorelli, Right Coast Hemp 22

CHAPTER 2:
HEMP BUILDING MATERIALS

• Leader Profile: Lucas Evans, E3 Agriculture 26

• Article: Hempcrete Adopted in Austin TX Residential Building Code 27

• Leader Profile: Morgan Tweet, IND HEMP 29

• Leader Profile: Melissa Nelson Baldwin, South Bend Industrial Hemp 32

• Listings: Hemp Processors 35

• Leader Profile: Zach Gill, Prairie Band Agriculture 38

• Leader Profile: Alex Wu, Kanda Hemp 40

• Leader Profile: Thomas Pires, Riverdale Hemp Gin 41

• Leader Profile: David Russell, CannaVision 42

• Listings: Hemp Suppliers Retail/Imports 43

• Leader Profile: Keith Dunn, East Coast Hemp Supply 46

• Listings: Lime Binder, Lime Supplies, Pozzolans 49

• Leader Profile Ryan Chivers, Earthaus Plasters 52

• Leader Profile: Dave Rosprim, Silacote 55

• Leader Profile: Cyril VanBatten, EcoStucco 56

• Listings: Plasters, Paints, Coatings & Tapes 57

• Listings: Equipment Sales Rental 59

CHAPTER 3:
SPECIALISTS

• Article: Hempcrete Fire-Testing Updates Approved for 2027 US Building Codes ... 63

• Leader Profile: Eric Milburn & Tanner Bowman, Healthy Hemp Homes 66

• Listings: Green Builders, Contractors ... 67

• Leader Profile: Jeremy Stephen, Evolve Construction ………………………………….. 75

• Leader Profile: Aaron Grail, Construction and Consulting …………. 76

• Leader Profile: David Hall, Hillside Center for Sustainable Living … 79

• Leader Profile: Phelan Dalton, Hemp Building Company ……………….. 80

• Leader Profile: Sergiy Kovalenkov, Hempire Holdings ……………………….. 83

• Leader Profile: John Hutton, Next Genesis Design ……………………… 84

• Listings: Hemp Building Consultants … 85

• Listings: Hemp Architects/Designers …87

• Leader Profile: April Magill, Root Down Designs ……………………… 94

• Leader Profile: Anthony Dente, PE, Verdant Structural Engineers ……… 96

• Leader Profile: Micaela Machado, Old Pueblo Hemp Co. ……………………. 97

• Leader Profile: Mark Benjamin, Crown Jade Design and Engineering …. 98

• Listings: Hemp Engineers ……………… 99

• Listings: Hemp Insulation Subcontractors, Installers ……………….. 101

• Leader Profile: Jared Sones & Tristin Wells, Victura Hemp …………………… 106

• Leader Profile: Cameron McIntosh, Americhanvre Cast Hemp ……………… 107

• Leader Profile: Navid Hatfield ………. 108

• Listings: Plasterers …………………… 109

• Listings: Financial Services, Transportation, Hemp Media/PR ……………………110

• Leader Profile: Danny Desjarlais, Lower Sioux Hemp/Green Buffalo Foundation ……………………………….. 111

• Leader Profile Johan Tjissen, HempBLOCK USA ……………………….. 112

CHAPTER 4:
HEMP PRODUCT MANUFACTURERS

• Article: Article: MN Adopts Hemp Building Codes ……………………………. 115

• Listings: Hemp Block Systems …….. 119

• Leader Profile: Zach Popp, Sativa Building Systems ………………… 121

• Listings: Hemp Panel Systems …….. 123

• Leader Profile: Gregory Wilson, HempWood ……………………………. 124

• Leader Profile: Matt Marino, Homeland Hempcrete …………………… 127

• Hemp Cement, Hemp Flooring/Hardwoods, Hemp OSB/Plywood/Fiberboard, Hemp Batt Insulation …………………. 128

• Leader Profile: Miles Gathright, Boardwurks ……………………………. 129

• Listings: Hemp Stains and Resins, Hemp Plastic ……………………………. 130

• Leader Profile: Chad Frey, Bison Biomaterials …………………….. 131

• Leader Profile: Matthew Mead, Hempitecture, Inc. ……………………….. 132

CHAPTER 5:
RESEARCHERS, ACADEMIC STUDIES, TESTING AGENCIES

• Listings: Academic Listings & Testing Agencies 134

• Article: NY Researchers Adapt Industrial Machinery for Plant Fibers 135

CHAPTER 6:
INTERNATIONAL HEMP BUILDERS & SUPPLIERS

• Australia 140

• Leader Profile: Klara Marosszeky, Australian Hemp Masonry Pty Ltd. 142

• Austria, Belgium, Bulgaria 145

• Leader Profile: Gaetan DuJardin, IsoHemp 146

• Canada 147

• Leader Profile: David Geertz, Renewabuild 149

• Costa Rica, Cypress, Czech Republic 150

• Article: Restoring the Ruined Portugal Village of Chumbaria 151

• Leader Profile: Ingmar Nopens, C-Biotech 154

• Denmark, Estonia 155

• France 156

• Leader Profile: Xavier Delacour, Quadra Concrete 157

• Leader Profile: Daniel Daviller, St. Astier/Construire en Chanvre 161

• Leader Profile: Susanne Bartholome, Merseburg U of Applied Sciences 167

• Germany, Hungary 168

• Leader Profile Gökcan Güney & Roger Bauer, DuraHemp 169

• Iceland, India, Ireland, Israel 170

• Italy, Japan, Latvia, Lithuania, Mexico 171

• Leader Profile Gaurav Dixit, GoHemp 172

• Nepal, Netherlands 173

• New Zealand 174

• Poland 175

• Portugal, Saudi Arabia, Serbia, Slovakia, Slovenia, South Africa 176

• Spain, Sweden, Switzerland, Thailand 177

• Ukraine, United Kingdom 178

• Leader Profile: Raquel Sanchis Ulacia, Hempcrete Spain 179

• Leader Profile: Ian Pritchitt, GreenCore Homes 181

HEMPSTEADS
ARCHITECTURAL DETAILS FOR
Hemp - Lime Construction
By Timothy Callahan

Order Here

Reviews for *Hempsteads*:

"Tim Callahan is a master design/builder with many built hempcrete projects under his belt. We owe him a debt for undertaking this work and sharing it with us here."- ***Clarke Snell, RA, Associate Professor of Architecture, NYIT***

"No other builder in North America, other than Tim Callahan, has successfully built hemp-lime residences in multi-hazardous regions (flooding, hurricanes, seismic)... He adeptly walks us through how to insulate with hemp-lime." - ***Kiko Thébaud, Architect***

INTRODUCTION

Once again, we're excited to welcome you back to Your Greenbuilt Revolution! As publishers of HempBuildMag.com, we are thrilled to bring a new and updated edition of the Hemp Building Directory for 2026.

We are watching the industry grow and expand in this comprehensive directory of the international hemp building industry in 2026. Our listings cover more than 800 unique companies and experts in 32 different countries in 28 categories.

If you are a professional builder looking to expand into the hemp space, you'll find the connections, suppliers and contacts you need here.

Everything you need is here in one convenient place: Hemp and lime suppliers, green builders, architects, engineers, plasterers and equipment are all here. Plus, you'll find a list of academic resources, and suppliers of hemp building products, from hemp blocks to plasters, stains, flooring, batt insulation and wallpaper.

Looking toward the future:

• More U.S. cities, states and jurisdictions are welcoming hemp-lime into residential building codes. Last year, we saw hemp-lime International Residential Code Appendix BL was adopted by the City of Austin, TX and the State of Minnesota.
• More international cooperation is taking place in the hemp-building industry with U.S. collaborations with experienced builders and architects from Belgium, France, Germany and Ukraine.
• Fire-resistant hemp building materials are increasingly the answer to climate extremes and natural disasters. Fire tests for ASTM E119 and E83 have shown that hemp-lime can withstand ignition – giving us the tools we need for fire resistant homes.
• Decarbonization a focus - Global focus on reducing embodied carbon in the built environment puts the spotlight on bio-based building materials like hempcrete, hemp batt insulation and hemp OSB. Carbon credits for bio-material buildings are being offered in the EU and will soon spread to the United States.

We are excited for the future of hemp building and construction, and we think you will be too.

Jean Lotus,
Publisher,
HempBuildMag.com.

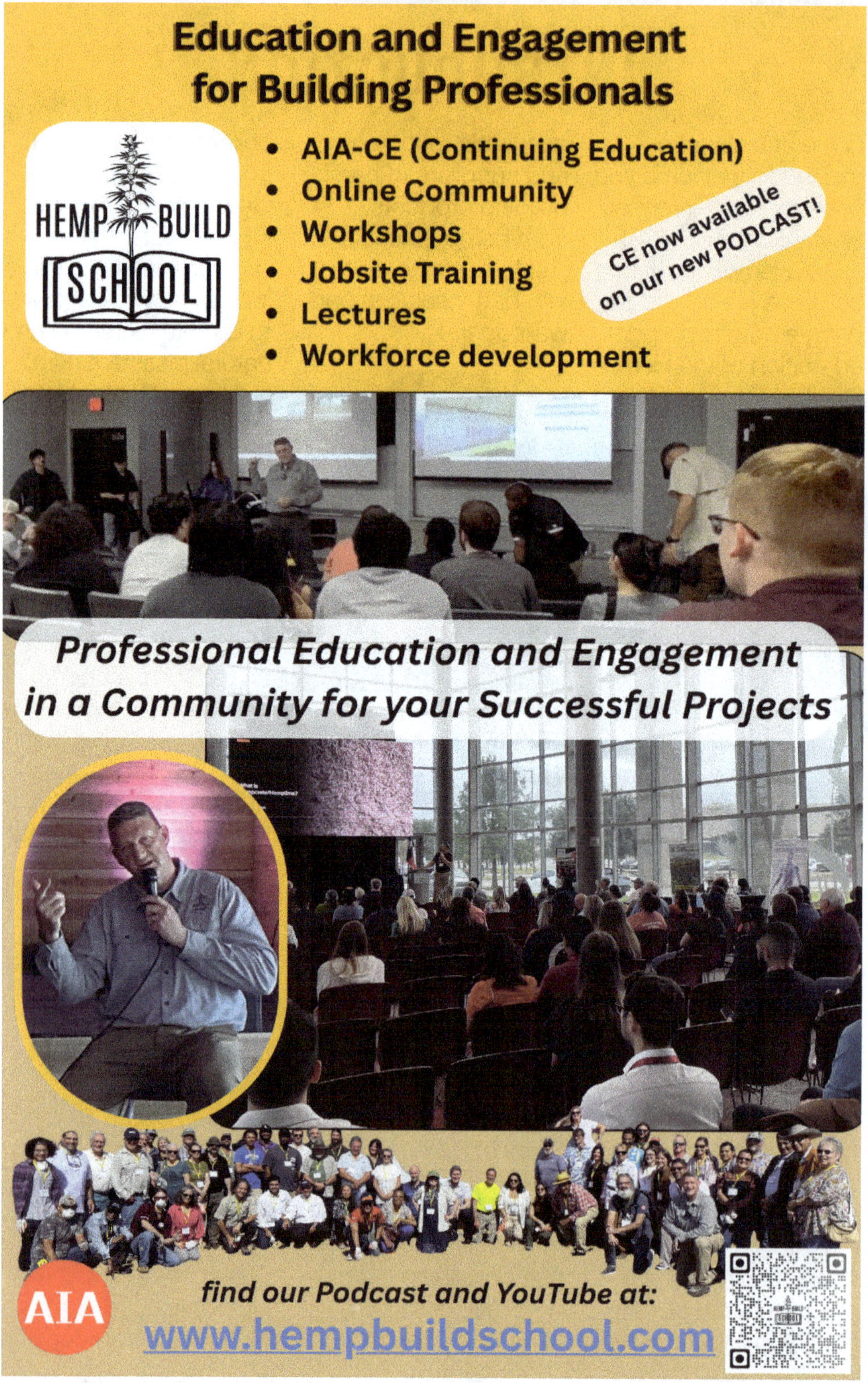
Education and Engagement
for Building Professionals
HEMP BUILD SCHOOL
AIA-CE (Continuing Education)
Online Community
Workshops
Jobsite Training
Lectures
Workforce development
CE now available on our new PODCAST!
Professional Education and Engagement
in a Community for your Successful Projects
AIA
find our Podcast and YouTube at:
www.hempbuildschool.com

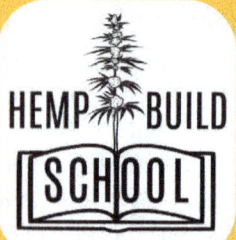

CHAPTER 1

EDUCATION

ADVOCACY

TRAINING

CA Hempcrete ADU Built with French Panel Prototypes

By Jean Lotus

Prefabricated panel hempcrete ADU in Eureka. Photo courtesy of Lisa Sundberg, *Indigenous Habitat Institute*.

On a chilly Pacific Redwoods morning in April, Joann Kerns, 68, was perched on her garage roof in Eureka, CA filming a crane installing the first 2,000 lb. wall panel for her new hempcrete ADU (accessory dwelling unit), when the operation took a surprising turn.

"The workers piled the panel onto the forklift held by these straps and they pulled it up and it started to spin," she told HempBuild Mag. Everyone watched as the panel came crashing down and smashed onto the ground, she said.

The five prefabricated panels for her new building had been transported 60 miles from the Hoopa Modular factory in Humboldt County where they were fabricated using a special imported lime binder formulated in France for large highrise hempcrete projects.

Kerns, her builder/engineer (and next-door neighbor) Chrissy Backman feared the worst – that the panel would be cracked or crumbled, causing delays on the new building.

But despite falling to the ground, the panel was unscathed.

Backman credited the French formulation for the panel's indestructibility.

"I'm an engineer, and I want to use material that I'm confident in," she said. "Respectable brands from France have done the fire testing, the seismic testing, they have specifications," she added.

"We had a sigh of relief," to find the panel was undamaged, she said, but the incident validated the decision to use specified products to create the best product for a modular housing prototype. The new 700 sq. foot ADU is the first permitted hempcrete structure in the NoCal City of Eureka and among the first prefabricated hempcrete panel projects in the state. The ground-breaking project was instigated by the Trinidad, CA-based Indigenous Habitat Institute (IHI).

IHI's founder, Lisa Sundberg, of Yurok descent and a member of the Trinidad Rancheria, has worked for several years with EU suppliers and experts with the goal of building a hempcrete panel factory on tribal land.

Partnering with Oregon State University, the institute was awarded a $630,000 grant last year to start the factory, working with the College of the Redwoods and bringing a knowledge transfer of hemp-lime technology and best practices from France.

"These materials have been tested in the EU," Sundberg said. "They've done the gauntlet run."

With a background in building energy analysis, and as a member of the California Coastal Commission, Engineer Backman had been looking for solutions to meet California's energy codes.

"You need continuous exterior insulation and the most prevalent material used is foam," Backman said. Petroleum-based spray foam insulation can release toxic gasses, especially when they burn. "So, how do we not use foam? That was my segue into hempcrete," she said.

The walls for the project were fabricated in a partnership with non-profit Building LIves by Building Structure where CEO Franklin Richards teaches construction at nearby College of the Redwoods.

The new build will "pave the way to scalability," Sundberg said. The next step will be College of the Redwoods taking on the accreditation of the French hempcrete training while IHI hosts workshops, she said. Long term, the goal is manufacturing binder in the USA and sourcing local hemp to localize the supply chains.

"We have the talent in our community to pull this off at a local level," Sundberg said.

JAMES KITCHIN
Systemic Changes will open the Door for More Bio-Based Materials

I work in the intersection between material systems and ecosystems, which leads me to focus on natural and bio-based materials. Most of my career as a structural engineer and design consultant has been based in Europe and Africa, where it is much easier to use bio-based materials.

When I arrived in the US in 2022 I was pleased to find so many bio-based material companies with products but I couldn't get them into our commercial-scale buildings that are working with tight budgets - we typically work with non-profit organizations.

There were lots of reasons why we were finding it difficult to implement these materials and it wasn't a design challenge, so MASS and New Frameworks co-founded the Bio-Based Materials Collective (BBMC) to try to address these systemic challenges. We are helping to build a movement around bio-based materials, facilitate collaboration between people, and engage parts of the wide material ecosystem – finance, governance, education, etc.

What was a win for your organization in the past year?
It was a sign that BBMC was having an impact when a BBMC 2025 Summit attendee came up to me at MASS's NYC Climate Week event to let me know they had collaborated with another BBMC member on a grant.

James Kitchin is director of the Abundant Futures Design Lab at MASS Architecture and co-founder of the Bio-Based Material Collective.

I work at a commercial building scale, so not single family residential. The first issue we come up against is building code. At a high level, we have building codes for public health, safety, and welfare. If we led with this, then we would also be thinking about the climate and nature-impacts of our materials, the toxicity for builders and users, and the long-term pollution impacts.

HEMP BUILDING DIRECTORY 2026

LEADER PROFILE

CLIFTON "RAY" KADERLi
Hemp Materials Ready to Move Forward at Scale

I founded my companies to support my own projects. I guide the effort and collaborate with contributors. Oceans of professional opportunity exist for designers, builders, subcontractors, suppliers, consultants, and others. Owners, and occupants will be the real winners, not just the marketplace.

I describe myself as a "brutally pragmatic" business professional. I am drawn to the long-term performance and efficiency of hemp-lime. Both are money in my pocket monthly. I also am an environmental steward with great joy about how economic and environmental objectives are not adversarial, but complementary. I am fond of saying "Hemp checks all the checkboxes."

The size and scale of the hemp supply chain participants right now shows how "ready" everything is to move forward at scale.

What was a win for your company in the past year?

Completing a permitted hempcrete house in San Antonio, and then refinancing it with a mortgage and insurance with no hassles.

What bottlenecks have you observed in the natural building industry and how would you solve them?

We need to show ourselves to production building and development as viable and ready. The market desire occurs naturally. Passing the scrutiny of the building industry that needs to perform in an environment of rigid accountability will happen as we build, build, build... and build systems to support the effort.

I am an entrepreneur and land steward at heart. I love to build long-term assets that also give opportunity of ownership to tenants. I will continue to build houses, and build businesses that support building houses with HEMP.

Ray Kaderli is founder of Hemp Build Network and co-founder of Hemp Build School, both based in New Braunfels, TX.

2026 | Hemp Building Directory **13**

EDUCATION • ADVOCACY • TRAINING

EDUCATION TRAINING AND ADVOCACY

AZ

OLD PUEBLO HEMP COMPANY - Tucson
Contact: Micaela Machado
Oldpueblohemp.com

CA

INDIGENOUS HABITAT INSTITUTE - Trinidad
Contact: Lisa Sundberg
Indigenoushabitatinstitute.com

COLLEGE OF THE REDWOODS - Eureka
Redwoods.edu

TINY HEMP HOMES - Riverdale
Contact: Wade Atteberry
Tinyhemphomes.com

CO

Featured

NATURALIA CONSTRUCTION - Alamosa
Contact: Gamal Jadue Zalaquette
(732) 239-3758
Naturaliaconstruction.com
610 State Ave, Alamosa, CO 81101
Gamal@naturaliaconstruction.com

Featured

HEMP BUILDING COMPANY - Lafayette
Contact: Phelan Dalton
(720) 231-6865
Hempbuildingco.com
Info@hempbuildingco.com

HIGH DESERT HEMP HOMES - Howard
Contact: Taylus Schley
Highdeserthemphomes.com

COLORADO GREEN BUILDING GUILD - Boulder
Contact: Shannon Wehner
Cgbg.org

NATURAL BUILDING ALLIANCE - Boulder
Contact: Jean Lotus
Natural-builing-alliance.org

REZOLANA INSTITUTE - San Luis
Contact: Arnie Valdez
Rezolana.av@gmail.com

ROCKY MOUNTAIN INSTITUTE (RMI) - Boulder
Contact: Chris Magwood
Rmi.org

Panelized hempcrete ADU in Eureka, CA built by Indigenous Habitat Institute. Photo courtesy of Lisa Sundberg.

EDUCATION • ADVOCACY • TRAINING

TINY HEMP HOUSES
- Fort Collins
Contact: John Patterson
Tinyhemphouses.com

US HEMP BUILDING ASSOCIATION *- Denver*
Contact: Ashley Stallworth
USHBA.org

DC
NATIONAL HEMP ASSOCIATION
Contact: Erica Stark
Nationalhempassociation.org

NATIONAL INDUSTRIAL HEMP COUNCIL
Contact: Patrick Atagi
Nihcoa.com

DE
Featured
HEMPBLOCK USA
Contact: Johan Tijssen
(855) 760-0756
Hempblockusa.com
16192 Coastal Highway,
Lewes, DE 19958

IA
TIM WHITE, NATURAL BUILDER *- Waukon*
Contact: Tim White
Texashealthyhomes.com

IL
IHRISE *- Maple Park*
Contact: Kelly Flynn
Ihrise.org

ILLINOIS HEMP GROWERS ASSOCIATION
- Argenta
Contact: Rachel Berry
IllinoisHGA.com

PINK HATS CONSTRUCTION
- Chicago
Contact: Traci Quinn
Pinkhatsconstructiondevgrp.com

US HERITAGE GROUP
- Franklin Park
Contact: Tai Olson
Usheritage.com

IN
MIDWEST HEMP COUNCIL *- Martinsville*
Contact: Jamie Campbell Petty
Midwesthempcouncil.com

KS
PLANTED ASSOCIATION OF KANSAS *- Topeka*
Contact: Kelly Rippel
Plantedks.org

KY
COVINGTON ACADEMY OF HERITAGE TRADES
- Covington
Contact: Diane McConnell
Heritagetradesacademy.com

LA
GRO ENTERPRISES
- New Orleans
Contact: Joel Holton
Groenterprises.biz

MA
BIO BASED MATERIALS COLLECTIVE *- Boston*
Contact: James Kitchin
Massdesigngroup.org/work/research/bio-based-materials-collective

The Howland Hempcrete House, Southampton MA. Photo courtesy of Village Carpentry & Landscaping Builders.

EDUCATION • ADVOCACY • TRAINING

HEMPSTONE LLC
- Hatfield
Contact: Tom Rossmassler
Hempstone.net

MI
ART FARM FENNVILLE
- Fennville
Contact: Christine Curri
Theartcoast.com

GREENHOME INSTITUTE
- Grand Rapids
Contact: Jose Reyna
Greenhomeinstitute.org

HEATSPRING *- Ann Arbor*
Contact: Brittany "Brit" Heller
Heatspring.com

HEMP4HUMANITY
- Detroit
Contact: Cody Ley
H4h.earth

MN
AGRICULTURAL UTILIZATION RESEARCH INSTITUTE (AURI)
- Crookston
Contact: Harold Stanislawski
AURI.org

GREEN BUFFALO INSTITUTE *- Morton*
Contact: Danny Desjarlais
Greenbuffaloinstitute.org

MT
HEMP EDUCATION AND MARKETING INITIATIVE (HEMI) *- Fort Benton*
Contact: Pierre Berard
Hempinitiatives.org

Hemp home in Cleburne, TX. Photo courtesy Andrew Hancock, Limelife Construction.

ND
Featured
HOMELAND HEMPCRETE
Contact: Matthew Marino
(701) 426-3796
Homelandhempco.com
551 Airport Rd, Bismarck, ND 58504
Matt@Homelandhempcrete.com

NJ
Featured
RIGHT COAST HEMP
Contact: Kristin Santorelli
908-783-0269
Rchemp.com
364 N Main St. Suite 1a
Manahawkin NJ 08050

NE
GENERAL HEMP CONSTRUCTION
- Denton
Contact: Tina Jones
generalhempconstruction@outlook.com

NM
REFUGE INDUSTRIAL HEMP BUILDING
- Albuquerque
Contact: Robin Elkin
Rbtrelknm6@gmail.com

EDUCATION • ADVOCACY • TRAINING

Hemp Studio Montgomery, TX. Photo courtesy of Jean Lotus.

ST. FRANCIS HOMELESSNESS CHALLENGE
- Taos
Contact: Amy Farah Weiss
Saintfrancischallenge.org

NY
BUILD GREEN NOW
- Kingston
Contact: Henry Gage, Jr.
Buildgreennow.net

PARSONS NEW SCHOOL HEALTHY MATERIALS LAB *- NYC*
Contact: Jonsara Ruth
Healthymaterialslab.org

YOUARETHECITY
- Brooklyn
Contact: Kaja Kühl
Youarethecity.com

OR
ECONEST BUILDING CO.
- Ashland
Contact: Robert LaPorte
econesthomes.com

GLOBAL HEMP INNOVATION CENTER
- Corvallis
Contact: Jeffrey Steiner
Agsci.oregonstate.edu/hemp

HEMPTOWN ON MAIN
- Jacksonville
Contact: Greg Flavell
Hemptownonmain.org

NORTHWEST ECOBUILDING GUILD
- Portland
Contact: Michael Niall
Ecobuilding.org

PERENNIAL BUILDING, LLC *- Sisters*
Contact: Karen Rugg
Perennialbuiliding.com

TERRA VIDA ACADEMY
- Vernonia
Contact: Jeff Walton
Terravidaacademy.com

PA
Featured
AMERICHANVRE CAST HEMP
Contact: Cameron McIntosh
(833) 443-6727
Americhanvre.com
1529 Brookside Road,
Allentown, PA 18106

BUILDING BIOLOGY INSTITUTE *- Pittsburgh*
Contact: Erik Rosen
Buildingbiologyinstitute.org

EDUCATION • ADVOCACY • TRAINING

COEXIST BUILD
- Blandon
Contact: Ana Konopitskaya
Coexist.build

CRAFTWORK TRAINING CENTER *- Telford*
Contact: Daniel Christiansen
Craftworktrainingcenter.com

DOWN TO EARTH DESIGN *- Fawn Grove*
Contact: Sigi Koko
Buildnaturally.com

GREEN BUILDING ALLIANCE *- Pittsburgh*
Contact: Jenna Cramer
GBA.org

PA INDUSTRIAL HEMP ENGINE *- Hazleton*
Contact: David Minnig
Paihe.org

PENNSYLVANIA HEMP INDUSTRY COUNCIL
Contact: Erica Stark
Pahempindustry.org

PENNSYLVANIA HOUSING RESEARCH CENTER
- University Park
Contact: Ali Memari
Phrc.psu.edu

RODALE INSTITUTE
- Kutztown
Contact: Ramon Madrid
Rodaleinstitute.org

SC
Featured
ROOT DOWN BUILDING COLLECTIVE
Contact: April Magill
(843) 252-0151
Rootdownbuildingcollective.org
PO Box 13945, Charleston, SC 29412
info@rootdowndesigns.com

AMERICAN COLLEGE OF THE BUILDING ARTS
- Charleston
Contact: Colby M. Broadwater
Acba.edu

TN
HAVEN EARTH TRADE SCHOOL
- Old Fort
Contact: River Richardson
havenearthtradeschool.net

HEMP ALLIANCE OF TENNESSEE
- Nashville
Contact: Frederick Cawthon
Yourhat.org

HEMP BUILDING INSTITUTE *- Nashville*
Contact: Jacob Waddell
Hempbuildinginstitute.org

Hempcrete brick workshop in Charleston, SC. Photo courtesy Root Down Building Collective.

EDUCATION • ADVOCACY • TRAINING

TX

Featured
HEMP BUILD SCHOOL
-New Braunfels
Contact: Ray Kaderli
(540) 664-6499
Hempbuildschool.com
New Braunfels, TX
Ray@hempbuildnetwork.com

CENTER FOR MAXIMUM POTENTIAL BUILDING SYSTEMS - *Austin*
Contact: Gail Vittori
Cmpbs.org

TEXAS COB CO
- Kingsbury
Contact: Simon Gonzalez
Simon@texascob.com

VT

YESTERMORROW DESIGN BUILD SCHOOL
- Waitsfield
Contact: Sarah Johnson
Yestermorrow.org

WA

Featured
NEXT GENESIS DESIGN
- White Salmon
Contact: John Hutton
(312) 339-8248
Nextgenesisdesign.com
8 Debo Road, White Salmon, WA 98672

HIGHLAND HEMP HOUSE - *Bellingham*
Contact: Pamela Bosch
Highlandhemphouse.com

Hemp home in Nickelsville, VA. Photo courtesy Americhanvre Cast Hemp.

LEADER PROFILE

LISA SUNDBERG
Grants will Fund Long-Awaited Initiatives

I am of Native Yurok descent and a member of the Trinidad Rancheria in Northern California. I am a visionary, activist, a bit of a strategist and love doing service for our community, especially during ceremony time.

My biggest success was helping develop an industry sector in Indian gaming in the early 90's. I've taken a few pages from these play books and applied them to our work in the hempcrete/hemp industry.

We were recently awarded a grant from our community called Redwood Region RISE from an anonymous donor. This grant finally provides Indigenous Habitat Institute with the funding freedom needed to advance several long-awaited initiatives.

Lisa Sundberg serves as the CEO of the Indigenous Habitat Institute (IHI), Trinidad, CA

> " *This grant finally provides Indigenous Habitat Institute with the funding freedom needed to advance several long-awaited initiatives.* "

Specifically, we will be able to:

- Work directly with Saint Astier, a major player in France who have already accomplished the 4-hour burn rating, earthquake and U-value test (R-Value). They are experienced in prefabricated walls and a great partner as we build out an industry model for regions starting in my back yard of Humboldt County in Northern California.

- Our architects will be creating home designs to develop a small-scale panel production model.

- We will be building a 400 sq. ft. cabin to be built at Sue-Meg State Park. This location is personally meaningful to me, as my mother served on the board that helped create a traditional Yurok Plank House village there. The cabin will use cladding inspired by the plank house.

HEMP CASITA TOUR
Across America

RIGHT COAST HEMP

SPONSOR OUR TOUR

- **Look for our Hemp Workshops**
- **Showcase the Casita at your own Site**

rightcoasthemp@gmail.com
908-783-0269
www.rchemp.com
www.hempcasita.com
www.hearts-of-mercy.org

A For-Profit + Nonprofit Collaboration Healing the Soil, Empowering our Youth, Growing the Future

OUR BRAND our story

HEARTS OF MERCY
Love in Action

LEADER PROFILE
KRISTIN ORR SANTORELLI
Education and Strong Collaborations are Key

As founder and visionary of Right Coast Hemp, I'm guiding the mission rooted in healing the soil through industrial hemp while reaching youth who will shape the future. Our work centers on educating and collaborating with farmers, architects, builders and educators to advance regenerative hemp agriculture and hemp-based construction.

Alongside my partner and adviser, Mike Mercadante, we turn vision into action. We are now collaborating with Hearts of Mercy, our nonprofit, to extend our impact to the next generation through youth-focused initiatives. We are and will be a part of the change!

Finding hemp growing on our Kansas farmland lit a spark! It opened a door revealing what nature can provide. We are continually amazed by hemp's ability to heal soil and to serve in so many arenas: agriculture, construction, environmental restoration and education. Hemp represents the bridge between healing the land and taking us all to a healthier future for the planet.

Our Hemp Casita, built at Kansas State University, continues to make the rounds, educating about hemp construction. We will host more workshops in 2026.

Kristin Orr Santorelli and Michael Mercadante are principals of Right Coast Hemp, based in Barnegat, NJ

The wind behind our company has been the incredible people and organizations we've encountered across the globe, individuals with loving hearts, open minds and shared desire to heal the land and uplift future generations.

We believe continued education and strong collaborations are key to building confidence, alignment, and momentum. We're excited to be part of this larger movement and the big picture ahead.

A Network of Professionals and Supply Resources

You will need ALL five components for a successful hemp project:

★ Architect
★ Engineer
★ Builder
★ Supplier
★ Subcontractor

HEMP BUILD NETWORK

We look forward to aligning all five stars for your successful projects

Schedule your FREE consultation

Call Us! 540 664-6499
or go to
www.hempbuildnetwork.com

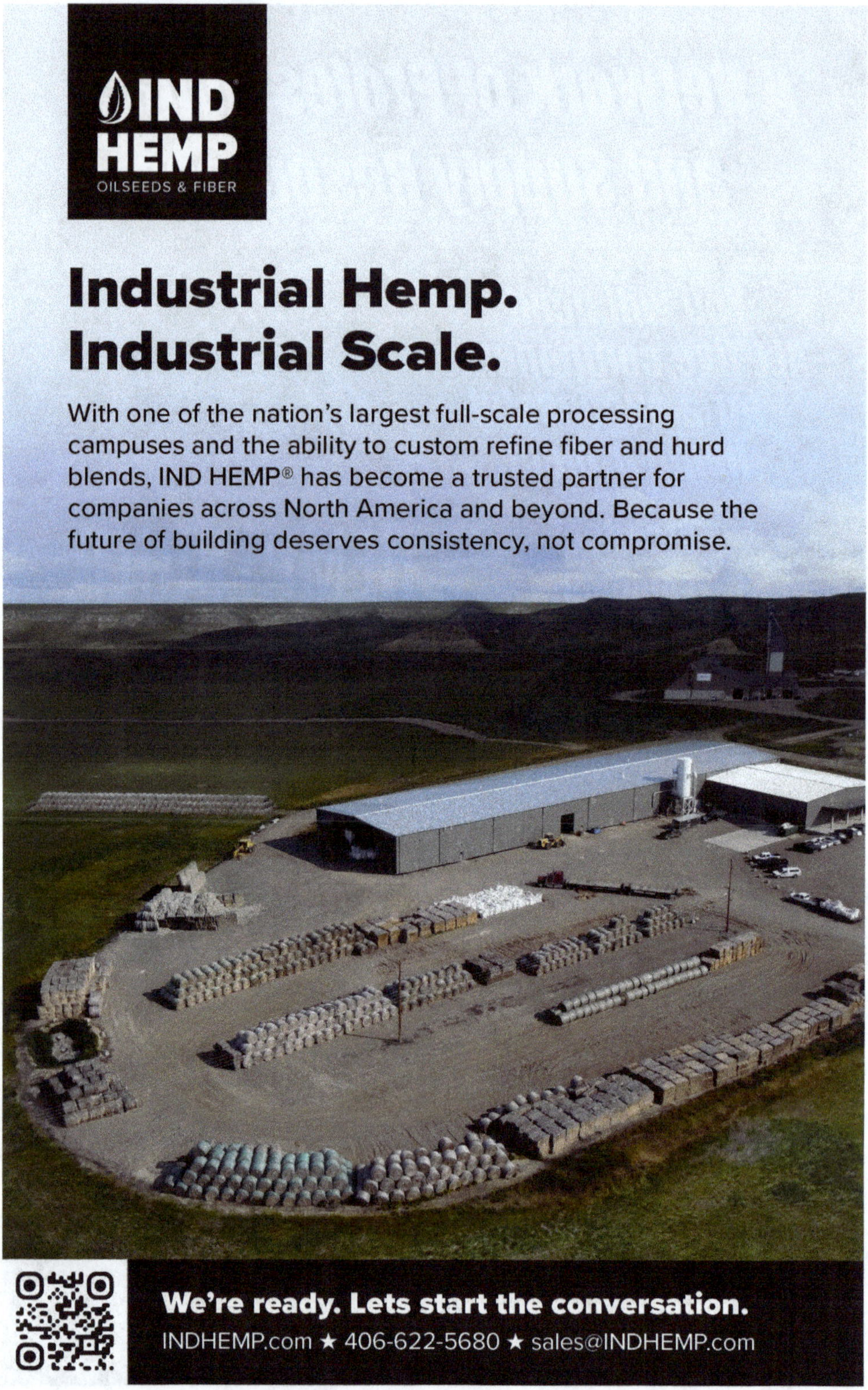

Industrial Hemp.
Industrial Scale.

With one of the nation's largest full-scale processing campuses and the ability to custom refine fiber and hurd blends, IND HEMP® has become a trusted partner for companies across North America and beyond. Because the future of building deserves consistency, not compromise.

We're ready. Lets start the conversation.
INDHEMP.com ★ 406-622-5680 ★ sales@INDHEMP.com

CHAPTER 2

HEMP BUILDING MATERIALS

LEADER PROFILE

LUCAS EVANS
Hemp Construction Boosts Farmers and Builders

Linking agriculture and construction to "grow homes" is akin to killing (saving) 2 birds with one stone! We're giving farmers endless demand, and builders sustainable and healthy alternatives. Industrial agriculture has the scale to compete with timber and fossil fuel-based building materials.

What was a win for your company in the past year?

We secured a long-term agreement on the Williamson County cotton gin facility, providing us the infrastructure and logistical hub to meet and maximize hemp demand and production for the State of Texas. Also we completed a hempcrete 3D printing project with Texas A&M.

What is something about hemp building/construction/processing you didn't know a year ago?

I learned hempcrete functions well without a coating or sheathing. While it is preferred we have had several examples of hempcrete being fully exposed to the elements and have seen little or no negative effects.

What bottlenecks have you observed in the industrial hemp industry and how would you solve them?

The further we get into this industry the more I realize how backwards our current finance and investment industry is. They have no framework or knowledge of a truly sustainable business and one that is beneficial for people and planet ... I'm increasingly spending more time with financiers and economists to help them understand and financialize what it looks like to grow homes.

Lucas Noble Evans is founder and CEO of Taylor, TX-based E3 Agriculture.

> " *Industrial agriculture has the scale to compete with timber and fossil fuel-based building materials.* "

Austin, TX Adopts Hempcrete in Local Building Codes

By Jean Lotus

Hempcrete designer/builder Tim Callahan, who co-authored the hemp-lime appendix in the 2024 International Building Code, addresses the crowd at a celebration of Austin's adoption of hempcrete into the local building codes. Photo courtesy of Jean Lotus.

In 2025, the city of Austin, TX officially adopted hempline (hempcrete) in the city's Building Technical Codes as an innovative building material to be used in local construction.

"Hempcrete offers a low-carbon alternative to traditional concrete and aligns with the city's broader goals to reduce greenhouse gas emissions in the building sector," a press release said.

The city adopted Appendix BL of the 2024 International Residential Code, "Hemp-Lime (Hempcrete) Construction," part of the model US residential building code which applies to homes and small multi-unit buildings.

Hempcrete, a mixture of hemp stalk hurds or "shiv" and lime binder, creates a long-lasting fibrous insulation wall assembly that makes an excellent insulation.

Because hemp sequesters carbon in the walls of a building, hempcrete is an excellent zero-carbon building material that can offset the construction industry's carbon footprint, supporters say.

"When it comes to our commitments around sustainability, we have to get creative, and hempcrete is more than just a greener building material—it's the type of efficient, innovative investment that reflects the kind of city we want to be," City of Austin Policy strategist John Lawler wrote in a note to city council members.

The amendment was supported by the American Institute of Architects' Committee on the Environment Austin branch, as well as city staff, Lawler said. "By embracing hempcrete, we can support local farmers and businesses, fostering economic opportunities within our community. …It's another example of how we can lead with both our innovation and intention," he added.

City Celebrates

Austin's Center for Maximum Potential Building Systems hosted a landmark event celebrating the city's formal adoption of hemp-lime. The evening also marked the official release of *Hempsteads: Architectural Details for Hemp-Lime Construction*, a new book by North Carolina–based architect and builder Tim Callahan.

Callahan, a co-author of Appendix BL and a long-time advocate of natural building, shared insight from decades of design experience and addressing the road ahead for biogenic building materials.

Callahan touched on the technical strengths of hemp-lime, including its resistance to mold, insects, and fire. "The alkalinity of lime — with a pH of 12 — makes it a very unfriendly environment for mold and insects," he said, while cautioning that no system is fail-proof. "It's not like if you use hempcrete, you'll never have any mold. Mold is everywhere… But this addresses the big ones — particularly in exterior walls."

"This is not just about a material," Callahan told the crowd. "It's about a systems shift — how we think about health, housing, and our responsibility to the planet."

"Buildings are living things," he added. "Everything is in a dynamic interaction with every other component." He likened the design process to conducting a symphony: "Everyone has to play their part at the right time… if it all is put together and blends in a way that's harmonious, then you have a building that is going to be sustainable over time."

The event in Austin, he said, felt like a kind of full-circle moment. "This feels to me like the completion of a dream, really… To see that a city like Austin has adopted this as part of their building code, and that you're all here interested in taking it forward, I think is just amazing."

LEADER PROFILE

MORGAN TWEET
Natural Fibers can Outperform Synthetics

Our company is a family-owned and vertically connected industrial hemp processor in Montana. My role is to steer long-term strategy—policy, market development, supply-chain partnerships, and grower relations—so that hemp becomes a reliable American rotation crop and a feedstock for next-generation materials.

Morgan Tweet is co-founder and CEO of Fort Benton, MT-based IND HEMP.

I'm drawn to hemp building because it sits at the intersection of agriculture, materials science, and climate resilience. Hemp fiber has the potential to replace carbon-intensive materials, strengthen rural economies, and open new revenue streams for growers. Seeing how hurd and fiber can be transformed into insulation, hempcrete, and composites makes this work feel both necessary and urgent.

What was a win for your company in the past year?

We've significantly expanded our engagement with builders and developers through our erosion control and landscaping products. It's not the flashy side of construction, but it's essential—and it's where hemp really shines.

What is something new about hemp building/construction/processing you didn't know a year ago?

Over the past year, I've learned how much fiber openness directly influences the thermal performance of hemp insulation. The way fiber is processed—how separated, "opened," and lofted it becomes—creates air pockets that dramatically improve R-values.

What bottlenecks have you observed in the industrial hemp industry and how would you solve them?

1. Limited education and market awareness among builders, architects, and developers.
2. Price competitiveness and inconsistent supply of fiber specific genetics.
3. Processing capacity constraints and lack of standardized fiber/hurd specifications.
4. Building-code approvals, testing requirements, and regulatory acceptance pathways.

CannaVision
GROWING A SUSTAINABLE FUTURE

Industrial Hemp Processing

Our PulseWave Natural Resonance Disintegration milling technology can reduce the size of hundreds of materials to microns in less than a second using the world's most innovative science at a fraction of the energy usage cost of standard impact mills.

FIBER	HURD	MICRONIZED	MICROFIBER	PELLETIZED
• Rope • Textiles	• Hemp Concrete • Absorbent Socks • Animal Bedding • Landscaping	• Bioplastics • 3D Printing • Cosmetics • Construction	• Textiles • Insulation	• Feed • Bedding • Cooking Fuel

"Let us supply your next project"

CannaVisionInc.com/Shop
(833) 284-4367

CannaVision, Inc. 777 Main Street, Suite 600, Fort Worth Texas 76102   (833) CVI-HEMP   (833) 284-4367
CANNAVISIONINC.COM

LEADER PROFILE
MELISSA NELSON BALDWIN
Developing the Industry and Farmers' Crop Portfolios

I provide agronomic support to our farmers growing to supply our processing facility. I also handle all social media content.

Hemp is intriguing to our team due to the versatility it allows for crop diversification as well products provided to consumers. We are a seed-to-final sale program, which allows us to really see the ramifications of each decision at every level and how it affects the downstream process.

Melissa Nelson Baldwin (Center) co-founder and research scientist of South Bend Industrial Hemp with partners Aaron Baldwin (L) and Richard Baldwin (R) in Great Bend, KS

developing the industry while also developing farmers' crop portfolios.

Processing continues to be an ever revolving door of learning. Our facility team does a great job of presenting ideas to increase throughput, while not sacrificing quality. It's been exciting watching our facility continue to hone in on what works for our customers.

What was a win for your company in the past year?

Having our first certified apprentice at the processing facility finish our program we set up through the Kansas Department of Commerce. We also contracted 4,000 acres of hemp across Kansas, Oklahoma, Texas and Colorado. We continue to grow while keeping quality high. Our focus has always been on

> " *Processing is a constant cycle of learning — improving throughput without ever sacrificing quality.* "

What bottlenecks have you observed in the industrial hemp industry and how would you solve them?

Sadly, we are still feeling the effects of uncertainty the CBD industry laid the foundation for in 2019. Education is the biggest bottleneck for us. How do we continue to educate on a mass scale about fiber production and remove the negative connotation of the cannabinoid industry? We continue to be a certified agritourism business, conduct over 100 tours a year, and are active on social media but there is still a large disconnect.

Prairie Band Agriculture

HEMP PROGRAM

785-364-2328

Prairie Band Ag
19035 US 75 Highway
Holton, KS 66436

EAST COAST
Hemp Supply Inc.

HEMPHURD, HEMPWOOD, HEMPWOOL

114 West Broad Street
Dunn, North Carolina 28334

910-237-1331

HEMP PROCESSORS

AK
SUNRAY HEMP - *Palmer*
Contact: Ray DePriest
sunrayhemp.com

AL
BASTCORE - *Montgomery*
Contact: Coleman Beale
Bastcore.com

CA
Featured
RIVERDALE HEMP GIN
- *Riverdale*
Westernfibers.com/riverdale-gin
Contact: Tom Pires
(918) 841-2289
PO Box 366
RIVERDALE, CA, 93656
Develop@WesternFibers.com

CO
GLOBAL FIBER PROCESSING
- *Monte Vista*
Contact: Craig Folmer
Globalfiberprocessing.com

NATUREA BIOMATERIALS - *Monte Vista*
Contact: Serge Buhkman
Natureabiomaterials.com

DE
Featured
KANDA HEMP
- *Wilmington*
Kandahemp.com
Contact: Alex Wu
(646) 705-9269
300 Delaware Ave, STE 210 #466, Wilmington, DE 19801
Alex@kandahemp.com

IA
HEMPAGRA - *Rock Valley*
Contact: Steve Voss
Hempagra.com

KS
Featured
SOUTH BEND INDUSTRIAL HEMP
- *Great Bend*
Southbendindustrialhemp.com
Contact: Melissa Nelson
(785) 851-0061
95 SW 20 RD, Great Bend, KS 67530
Southbendhemp@gmail.com

Featured
PRAIRIE BAND AGRICULTURE - *Holton*
prairiebandag.com
19035 US Highway 75, Holton, KS 66436
Contact: Zach Gill
(785) 364-2328
Zach.gill@prairiebandllc.com

Skid steer mixer for hempcrete. Photo courtesy of Tim Callahan.

HEMP PROCESSORS

Hemp blocks. Photo courtesy of Ray Kaderli.

MIDWEST HEMP TECHNOLOGIES
- Augusta
Contact: Sarah Stephens
Midwesthemptech.com

MO
TIGER FIBER HEMP
- St. Louis
Contact: James Forbes
Tigerfiberhemp.com

MIDWEST NATURAL FIBER *- St. Louis*
Contact: Patrick Van Meter
Midwestnaturalfiber.com

MN
GREEN FOX LLC
- South Haven
Contact: Ellie Fox
Greenfoxcompanies.com

HEMP ACRES *- Waconia*
Contact: Charles Levine
Hempacresusa.com

LOWER SIOUX HEMP
- Morton
Contact: Danny Desjarlais
Lowersioux.com

PRAIRIE PRODUCERS
- Olivia
Contact: Tim Seehusen
Prairieproco.com

MT
Featured
IND HEMP
Indhemp.com
Contact: Morgan Tweet
(406) 622-5680
1210 22nd St, Fort Benton, MT 59442
Sales@indhemp.com

NC
BIOPHIL NATURAL FIBERS *- Lumberton*
Contact: David Camby
Biophilfibers.com

NE
CONSOLIDATED CARBON *- Culbertson*
Contact: John Lupien
Consolidatedcarbon.com

HEMP PROCESSORS

ND
DAKOTA HURD CO
- *Wahpeton*
Contact: Justin Berg
Dakotahurd.com

NY
GREENE ACRES
- *Utica-Rome*
Contact: Hailee Greene
Greeneacresprocessing.com

PA
I-HEMP KATALYST
- *Hazleton*
Contact: Duane Shugars
I-hempkatalyst.com

SD
COMPLETE HEMP PROCESSING - *Winfred*
Contact : Ken Meyer
Completehempprocessing.com

DAKOTA HEMP
- *Wakonda*
Contact: Jonathan Peterson
Dakotahemp.com

TX
Featured
CANNAVISION, INC
- *Fort Worth*
cannavisioninc.com
Contact: David Russell
(833) 284-4367
4501 CR 312 B, Cleburne, TX 76431
Ihp@cannavisioninc.com

Featured
E3 AGRICULTURE
- *Taylor*
E3Agriculture.com
Contact: Lucas Evans
(512) 968-7904
308 Sturgis Street, Taylor, TX
Lucas@e3ag.world

DELTA AG PARTNERS
- *Dallas*
Contact: John Paul Merrit
Deltaag.com

ENVIRONMENTAL LIVING INDUSTRIES
- *Dumas*
Contact: Bryan Wilson
Eli.inc

PANDA BIOTECH
- *Wichita Falls*
Contact: Dixie Carter
Pandabiotech.com

TETRA HEMP COMPANY, LLC
- *Harlingen*
Contact: John Bradley
Tetrahempco.com

VA
PURE SHENANDOAH HEMP - *Elkton*
Contact: Jake Johnson
Pureshenandoah.com

WY
WYOMING HEMP CO
- *Hawk Springs*
Contact: Justin Loeffler
Wyominghemp.us

BUILD WITH PLANTS.
BUILD FOR THE FUTURE.

HEMPCRETE SOLUTIONS & PRODUCT DEVELOPMENT

Explore hempcrete at E3Agriculture.com

LEADER PROFILE

ZACH GILL
Specs and Consistency are Key in Hemp Processing

PBAG operates the largest industrial hemp processing facility in Kansas, not just in terms of throughput capacity, but also in overall facility size and equipment depth. We run a level of processing infrastructure that allows us to handle large volumes of material while maintaining quality and repeatability. We're also the only hemp processor in Kansas currently producing bioplastic-based products, which pushes us beyond raw-material processing.

Hemp is a material that connects agriculture, construction, and sustainability in a tangible way. Hemp gives us a chance to rethink how buildings are made, how materials are sourced, and how rural and Tribal communities can be part of that value chain.

What was a win for your company in the past year?

One of our biggest wins this past year was tightening the link between what happens in the field and what happens in the facility. By paying closer attention to how we grow,

Zach Gill is the production manager at Prairie Band Agriculture, based in Holton, KS.

harvest, store, and process hemp, we've been able to improve consistency and reliability across the board.

I didn't realize how much success in hemp building comes down to discipline and process rather than innovation alone. The material itself is solid, but it only performs well when the entire chain from farming practices to processing and handling is dialed in.

If the goal is construction, bioplastics, or other industrial applications, the specs need to be clear from the start. How it's grown, how it's harvested, how it's processed, and how it's stored. That requires tighter communication, fewer assumptions, and more long-term partnerships instead of spot transactions.

> **"** *The material itself is solid, but it only performs well when the entire chain from farming practices to processing and handling is dialed in.* **"**

HEMP BUILDING DIRECTORY 2026

LEADER PROFILE

ALEX WU
Hemp Can Lead to Material Decarbonization at Scale

I lead Kanda Hemp's seed strategy, supplying reliable, high-performing genetics and agronomy support so growers and processors consistently produce quality fiber and hurd. We also support hemp success through harvesting and processing solution partnerships.

I'm most interested in turning hemp fiber and hurd into standardized feedstocks for building materials and biocomposites—beyond just textiles. With consistent specs, hemp can replace key inputs in insulation, hempcrete, panels, and composite reinforcements. The bigger opportunity is material decarbonization at scale: shifting from petroleum/mineral-based materials to renewable, regionally produced inputs without sacrificing performance.

In the past year 2025, we raised seed quality to a new level since 2021—delivering better seed quality and crop performance results across the country. The win is simple: happier growers and processors, and we're proud to contribute to domestic fiber production.

What is something about hemp building/construction/processing you didn't know a year ago?

I didn't realize how quickly code acceptance is tightening around proof—especially fire-rated wall assemblies and Appendix BL adoption—and how that forces real standardization in both material specs and construction detailing

Alex Wu is founder and president of Kanda Hemp Seeds.

What bottlenecks have you observed in the industrial hemp industry and how would you solve them?

The bottleneck is that downstream products and specs aren't standardized yet, so demand is fragmented and processors can't run consistently. The solution is focused product development around a few proven applications, published specs, and multi-year offtake partnerships to create repeatable demand.

> " *The real opportunity for hemp isn't textiles—it's decarbonizing building materials at scale with standardized, performance-proven fiber and hurd.* "

LEADER PROFILE
THOMAS PIRES
Hemp Farming is Financially Competitive

At the Riverdale Hemp Gin, we engineered the modification of a standard processing cotton gin to process hemp stalk - separating the hemp bast fiber from the hemp hurd and then further processing the bast fiber by combing and further mechanically cleaning the hemp fiber that ranges from 1 ½ to 8 inches in length. The hemp hurd is hammermilled into lengths of 0.6mm to 18mm as determined by the customer needs; then further cleaned of residual bast fiber and dust to meet the customer needs.

As a farmer, and now a hemp processor of hemp products, I really value growing fiber hemp for several reasons: Hemp is a very easy crop to grow; no herbicides or insecticides needed, also hemp is very irrigation water efficient (I use drip irrigation). Using my cultural farming practices, hemp farming is financially (net margin) comparable to other annual crops grown in our farming area of California.

I am very interested in hempcrete and other natural material building construction. I am currently moving forward with a low-income housing project in Huron, California.

A win for my company during this past year is my decision to move forward with the development of the housing project in Huron, Ca., using green building materials.

The bottlenecks or delays when using natural building materials include finding qualified people with the knowledge to plan, engineer, and design a building project and complete all phases of the construction process from start to completion.

Thomas Pires is a partner of the Riverdale Hemp Gin in Riverdale CA.

HEMP BUILDING DIRECTORY 2026

LEADER PROFILE

DAVID RUSSELL
Precision Processing is a Game Changer for Industry

My work focuses on turning industrial hemp into scalable, high-value materials for construction, manufacturing, and sustainable fuel applications.

Industrial hemp isn't just a sustainable crop; it's a platform material. Hemp can be processed into fiber, hurd, cellulose, oils, resins, and carbon-rich feedstocks that touch everything from construction and packaging to composites, 3D printing, and even energy. Few plants offer that kind of versatility with such a small environmental footprint. Hemp becomes a serious alternative to petrochemical plastics, fiberglass, and other resource-intensive materials.

What was a win for your company in the past year?

Our biggest win this past year was moving from proof-of-concept to real-world production pathways.

Our Pulsewave technology advanced our ability to process hemp into high-purity fibers and biopolymer-ready feedstocks, which opened doors in areas like bioplastics, composite materials, and additive manufacturing. That shift takes hemp out of the niche category and into industrial-scale material science, which is where it belongs.

Just as important, we strengthened partnerships with manufacturers and technology developers who understand that hemp is the next generation of industrial input.

David Russell is the CEO of CannaVision, based in Fort Worth, TX.

A year ago, I didn't fully appreciate how sensitive material quality is to processing precision.
We tend to talk about hemp as a single material, but in reality, the micron size, fiber length, moisture content, and purification level completely change what the material can do.

Hemp's future is in more than farming and basic processing. It's in advanced processing and material science, where consistency and quality unlock entire industries.

HEMP SUPPLIERS/RETAIL/IMPORTS

CA
HEMP TRADERS
- *Los Angeles*
Contact: - Lawrence Serbin
Hemptraders.com

CO
Featured
HEMP BUILDING COMPANY - *Lafayette*
Hempbuildingco.com
Contact: Phelan Dalton
(720) 231-6865
Info@hempbuildingco.com

DC
Featured
BISON BIOCOMPOSITES
Bisonbiocomposites.com
Contact: Chad Frey
402-650-5032
318 Massachusetts Ave NE,
Washington, DC 20002
Info@bisonbiocomposites.com

FL
HURDZ HEMP
- *Wellington*
Contact: John Dunn
Hurdzhemp.com

ID
Featured
HEMPITECTURE, INC.
Hempitecture.com
Contact: Mattie Mead
(208) 218-8698
421 E 500 S #100, Jerome, ID 83338
Mattie@hempitecture.com

LA
DELTA AGROFIBER SOLUTIONS - *Mandeville*
Contact: Shawn Ledig
Deltaagrofiber.com

MI
CHANVRA MATERIALS
- *Allegan*
Contact: Brian Mogli
Chanvra.org

KANAF PARTNERS USA
- *Onaway*
Contact: Bob Lawrason
Kenafpartnersusa.com

MN
WINONA'S HEMP FARM
- *Osage*
Contact: Winona LaDuke
Winonashemp.com

MO
HEMP SOLUTIONS
- *Lexington*
Contact: Sally Virag Rivers
Hempsolutionsmo.com

Hempcrete installer Aaron Grail loads hemp into a mixer in Drake CO. Photo courtesy of Jean Lotus.

HEMP SUPPLIERS/RETAIL/IMPORTS

Insulating a Montana concrete block garage with hempcrete. Photo courtesy Americanvre.

NC
Featured
EAST COAST HEMP SUPPLY INC. - *Dunn*
Contact: Keith Dunn
Eastcoasthempsupply.com
(910) 237-1331
114 West Broad St, Dunn, NC 28334
Keith@eastcoasthempsupply.com

NV
BULK HEMP WAREHOUSE - *Pahrump*
Contact: Tyler Hoff
Bulkhempwarehouse.com

OR
HEMP SOLUTIONS OREGON - *Damascus*
Contact: Gary Lyman
Lymabeans@msn.com

HEMPTOPIA - *McMinnville*
Contact: Ty Frank
Hemptopia.com

PERENNIAL BUILDING, LLC
Contact: Karen Rugg
Perennialbuilding.com

PA
Featured
AMERICHANVRE CAST HEMP
Americanvre.com
Contact: Cameron McIntosh
(833) 443-6727
1529 Brookside Road,
Allentown, PA 18106
Cameron@americhanvre.com

HEMP ALTERNATIVE - *Kennett Square*
Contact: Michael Hudock
Hemp-alternative.com

TX
Featured
HEMP BUILD NETWORK
Hempbuildnetwork.com
Contact: Ray Kaderli
(540) 664-6499
New Braunfels, TX

CHANVRA MATERIALS - *Austin*
Contact: Frank Cheff
Chanvra.org

CONSOLIDATED CARBON - *Austin*
Contact: Jona Williams
Consolidatedcarbon.com

VA
OLD DOMINION HEMP - *Waynesboro*
Contact: Marty Phipps
Odhemp.com

THE SEED BEHIND YOUR BUILDING SUPPLY

Industrial hemp seeds bred for fiber & hurd production
Trusted by growers across the US since 2021

- **Proven Performance:** across US growing regions
- **Agronomy Support:** planting to harvest
- **Equipment Solutions:** harvest & decortication

Empower hemp growers to succeed—building a sustainable future

kandahemp.com
sales@kandahemp.com

LEADER PROFILE

KEITH DUNN
Hempcrete Innovation Could Open Vast New Opportunities

I merge my farming roots with my background in biology and chemistry from East Carolina University to support regional farmers and revive the hemp industry. Our retail store serves as a marketplace for emerging hemp products, including construction materials, helping to raise awareness of sustainable alternatives.

I am fascinated by how hemp connects row crop farmers to the construction industry. It is rewarding to see a locally grown crop turn into eco-friendly building materials that boost rural economies while reducing environmental impact.

What was a win for your company in the past year?

We developed relationships with financial and educational institutions to establish a regional industrial hemp supply chain. We are also proud to have several grant proposals accepted for consideration, marking a significant step toward a stronger local ecosystem.

What is something about hemp/natural building/construction/processing you didn't know a year ago?

I learned about innovations aimed at making hempcrete load-bearing. This development could expand its use beyond non-structural applications, opening up vast new opportunities in construction.

Keith Dunn is founder and CEO of East Coast Hemp Supply, based in Dunn, NC.

What bottlenecks have you observed in the natural building industry and how would you solve them?

The primary bottleneck is limited access to consistent, processed hemp materials at scale. We aim to solve this by establishing a local scutching facility to supply clean long-staple fiber, short fiber, and hurd directly to builders, reducing reliance on traditional materials.

SILACOTE

Environmentally Safe Inorganic Paints

Bring hempcrete and natural plasters to life with Silacote, the mineral paint that breathes with your building.

- Non-toxic
- Non-combustible - does not burn
- Naturally compatible with earth and lime plasters
- Versatile and easy to use

- 282 nature-inspired colors
- 100% vapor-open & zero VOCs
- Durable, light, fast, and petroleum-free

Color beautifully. Build naturally.

Visit silacote.com

800-249-1881

LIME BINDER, LIME SUPPLIES, POZZOLAN

AL
CHENEY LIME & CEMENT CO. - *Allgood*
Contact: Rick Townson
Cheneylime.com

AZ
OLD PUEBLO HEMP CO. - *Tucson*
Contact: Micaela Machado
Oldpubelohemp.com

CA
HEMP TRADERS - *Los Angeles*
Contact: - Lawrence Serbin
Hemptraders.com

TRANSMINERAL, USA - *Petaluma*
Contact: Michel Couvreux
Lime.us

HEMPCEMENT CO. - *Newport Beach*
Contact: Serena Overhoff
Hempcement.co

CO
Featured
HEMPIRE HOLDINGS CO
Magic Minerals
Hempire.tech
Contact: Sergiy Kovalenkov
+38 0676585350

Featured
HEMP BUILDING COMPANY - *Lafayette*
Hempbuildingco.com
Contact: Phelan Dalton
(720) 231-6865
Info@hempbuildingco.com

COLORADO LIME COMPANY - *Delta*
Contact: John Gagnon
Uslm.com/USLM_Colorado

ID
Featured
HEMPITECTURE, INC.
Hempitecture.com
Contact: Mattie Mead
(208) 218-8698
421 E 500 S #100, Jerome, ID 83338
Mattie@hempitecture.com

IL
US HERITAGE GROUP
Usheritage.com
Contact: Tai Olson

IA
ILC RESOURCES - *Cloverdale*
Contact:
Ilcresources.com

MO
MISSISSIPPI LIME - *Genevieve*
Contact: Ted Frey
Mississippilime.com

OH
GRAYMONT - *Genoa*
Contact: Todd File
Graymont.com

OR
PERENNIAL BUILDING, LLC - *Sisters*
Contact: Karen Rugg
Perennialbuilding.com

A workshop participant cuts a hempcrete block with a chainsaw at the HempBLOCK USA master builder workshop in Wildwood, GA. Photo courtesy of Crystal Cervantez-Tkac.

LIME BINDER, LIME SUPPLIES, POZZOLAN

Hempcrete home in Drake, CO. Photo courtesy of Jean Lotus.

PA

Featured
AMERICHANVRE CAST HEMP
Americhanvre.com
Contact: Cameron McIntosh
(833) 443-6727
1529 Brookside Road, Allentown, PA 18106

CARMEUSE LIME & STONE - *Pittsburgh*
Contact: Matt Benusa
Carmeuse.com

LANCASTER LIMEWORKS
- *Lancaster*
Contact: Jonathan Owens
Lancasterlimeworks.com

LIMEWORKS US
- *Telford*
Contact: Daniel Christiansen
Limeworks.us

SAINT-GOBAIN NORTH AMERICA - *Malvern*
Contact: Dennis Wilson
Saint-gobain-northamerica.com

SD

PETE LIEN & SONS
- *Rapid City*
Contact: Daryl Mecham
Petelien.com

TX

Featured
E3 AGRICULTURE
- *Taylor*
E3Agriculture.com
Contact: Lucas Evans
(512) 968-7904
308 Sturgis Street, Taylor, TX
Lucas@e3ag.world

LIME BINDER, LIME SUPPLIES, POZZOLAN

Featured
HEMP BUILD NETWORK
- New Braunfels, TX
Contact: Ray Kaderli
(540) 664-6499

AUSTIN WHITE LIME CO. *- Austin*
Contact: Bud Baranek
Austinwhitelime.net

BIOLIME *- Woodway*
Contact: Brian Coia
Biolime.com

LHOIST NORTH AMERICA
- Fort Worth
Contact: Lindsey Geeslin
Lhoist.com

US LIME & MATERIALS
- Dallas
Contact: John Gagnon
Uslm.com

UT
ECO MATERIAL TECHNOLOGIES
- South Jordan
Contact: Grant Quasha
Ecomaterial.com

WV
GREER LIME CO
- Riverton
Contact: Kyle Apple
Greerlime.com

Hempcrete blocks installed in Tucson at Camp Cooper by Old Pueblo Hemp Co. Photo Courtesy of Micaela Machado.

HEMP BUILDING DIRECTORY 2026

LEADER PROFILE

RYAN CHIVERS
Regenerative, Biobased Materials Represent the Future of Building

I'm the owner and founder of Earthaus, a manufacturer of durable, accessible lime plasters sourced and made in the US. I began as a plasterer in 1999 working on straw bale homes, began formulating lime plasters in 2005, and launched what is now Earthaus Plaster in 2018. This past year we launched Earthaus BUILD, a line of specialized plasters for natural building applications.

What most interests you about hemp and biobased construction?

I'm inspired by regenerative, biobased materials because they represent the future of building—materials that actively improve human health and the environment. Hemp, in particular, inspires me for its remarkable carbon-sequestering capacity, its ability to grow quickly in diverse climates, and how wonderfully compatible it is with lime plaster! I'm especially interested in hemp block and prefab panel systems for their potential to scale biobased building into mainstream construction.

Ryan Chivers is co-owner and product developer for Earthaus Plaster.

What bottlenecks have you observed in the natural building industry and how would you solve them?

After 25 years in natural building, the biggest challenge I see is the lack of standardized materials and systems. For hemp and other bio-based methods to gain wider acceptance among mainstream builders and code officials, we need consistency and clear standards just like in conventional construction. That's what we set out to achieve with Earthaus BUILD: standardized interior and exterior lime plaster systems for biobased and earthen construction. Our BUILD Plaster System for hempcrete is suitable for cast, block, spray, and panel applications. Each Earthaus Plaster is expertly formulated and precisely mass manufactured, available at scale, and supported with standardized mineral pigment colors, finish options, and technical documentation to ensure success from installation through long-term performance.

DAVID ROSPRIM

Hemp Building is Being Adopted as a Viable Material Alternative in Many Environments

The versatility & creativity of using these earth-based materials is demonstrated by the increasing adoption of eco-friendly construction methods, including hempcrete.

What was a win for your company in the past year?

We've noticed increasing awareness by builders of the versatility, durability and benefits offered by our silicate mineral paint when paired with natural renewable building materials.

What is something about hemp building/construction/processing you didn't know a year ago?

How quickly it is being adopted as a viable building alternative in a broad range of environments.

> " The versatility & creativity of using these earth-based materials is demonstrated by the increasing adoption of eco-friendly construction methods "

David Rosprim is president and co-founder of Silacote, located in California and BC, Canada.

HEMP BUILDING DIRECTORY 2026

LEADER PROFILE

CYRIL VANBATTEN
Hemp-Lime Adoption Requires a Systems Standarization

I represent a lineage of expertise in architectural natural lime plasters and binders that dates to 1785. Since introducing our world-class knowledge to the US market in 2004, our mission has been to provide a sustainable alternative to Portland cement and synthetic stuccos.

Our ecostucco® product provides a comprehensive, fully vetted finish system engineered for consistent and reliable interior and exterior lime plaster solutions, specifically optimized for integration with bio-based and earthen construction substrates.

Unlike modern, petrochemical-based structures that often restrict vapor exchange, hemp-lime naturally regulates heat and moisture by allowing water vapor to pass freely. This inherent quality, especially when paired with our lime plasters and binders, aligns exceptionally well with biophilic and wellness-driven design principles.

Hemp-lime's widespread adoption remains severely hampered by how it integrates—or rather, fails to integrate—within the current, highly standardized construction framework, especially from an architect's perspective, who must manage the entire process: specification, design, approval, construction, and, ultimately, scaling.

Cyril Vanbatten is founder of ecostucco®, based in San Rafael, CA.

For over three decades, those committed to the field of natural and bio-based building have faced a consistent and significant hurdle: the fundamental lack of material and system standardization. While the benefits of materials like hempcrete—from superior thermal performance to carbon sequestration—are undeniable, their widespread adoption remains bottlenecked by the absence of the clear, consistent standards that govern conventional construction. We must establish the same level of consistency, predictability, and rigorously documented performance that defines traditional building materials.

PLASTERS, PAINTS, COATINGS, TAPES

Featured
EARTHHAUS PLASTER
- *Duluth, MN*
Earthausplaster.com
Contact: Ryan Chivers
(800) 917-2414
Admin@earthausplaster.com

Featured
ECOSTUCCO (MEDITER-RANEAN COLORS, LLC)
- *San Rafael, CA*
Ecostucco.com
Contact: Cyril Vanbatten
(415) 455-9896
3060 Kerner Blvd, Ste S, San Rafael, CA 94901
Info@ecostucco.com

Featured
SILACOTE (GSM ASSOCIATES, LLC)
- *Grass Valley, CA*
Silacote@silacote.com
Contact: David Rosprim
(800) 249-1881
111 Bank St. #153, Grass Valley, CA 95945

475 HIGH PERFORMANCE BUILDING SUPPLY - *Brooklyn, NY*
Contact: Floris Keverling Buisman
475.supply

AMERICAN CLAY PLASTERS
- *Albuquerque, NM*
Contact: Croft Elsaesser
Americanclay.com

Ryan Chivers of Earthaus mixes lime plaster in Bozeman, MT. Photo courtesy Jean Lotus.

QUADRA

French Manufacturer of Hempcrete Block Machine

TURN KEY PRODUCTION UNITS DEDICATED TO THE MANUFACTURE OF HEMP BLOCKS AND BIO-SOURCED PRODUCTS

QUADRA

40 route de Findrol
Contamine-sur-Arve
France
Tel. +33 4 50 03 92 21
www.quadra-concrete.com

INNOVATIVE AND STATE-OF-THE-ART EQUIPMENT FOR HIGH QUALITY PRODUCTS

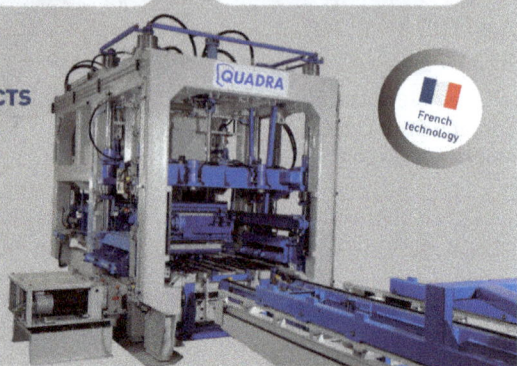

French technology

EQUIPMENT SALE/RENTAL

AZ
Featured
QUADRA CONCRETE USA
Quadra-concrete.com
Contact: Pascal Allain
(602) 373-2951
One Renaissance Tower 2, N. Central Avenue Suite #1800
Phoenix, AZ 85004
Info@quadra-concrete.com

CO
Featured
HEMP BUILDING COMPANY - *Lafayette*
Contact: Phelan Dalton
Hempbuildingco.com

PA
Featured
AMERICHANVRE CAST HEMP
Americhanvre.com
Contact: Cameron McIntosh
(833) 443-6727
1529 Brookside Road,
Allentown, PA 18106

LIMEWORKS US
- Telford
Contact: Daniel Christiansen
Limeworks.us

Hempcrete tip up panel 11 unit project at Hillside Center for Sustainable Living, Newburyport MA. Photo courtesy of Americhanvre.

Highland Hemp House in Bellingham WA. Courtesy of Highland Hemp House

CHAPTER 3
SPECIALISTS

AARON GRAIL

Consulting | Construction
West Coast HEMP-Lime Construction
aarongrailconstruction.com
707 292 4097

Hempcrete Fire-Testing Updates Approved for 2027 US Building Codes

By Jean Lotus and Martin Hammer

Hempcrete code warriors (L-R) Cameron McIntosh, Martin Hammer and Anthony Dente attended ICC Public Hearings in Cleveland last year. Photo courtesy of Cameron McIntosh

Hemp-lime (hempcrete) construction in US residential building codes took a major step forward in Cleveland last fall when proposed updates to Appendix BL of the 2027 International Residential Code (IRC) were unanimously approved during the International Code Council (ICC) Committee Week. An online fundraiser successfully raised more than $12,000 to pay for the code adoption.

It's an important milestone for hemp-lime construction in the United States because the updated codes will include fire-rated walls in the appendix. Hemp-lime construction was first approved for the 2024 IRC.

Architect Martin Hammer and engineer Anthony Dente, both based in Berkeley, CA, joined Cameron McIntosh, a Pennsylvania-based hempcrete subcontractor and founder of Americhanvre Cast Hemp, to submit the updates before the IRC committee, which approved the changes 11-0.

"Although inclusions like these may seem obvious to those of us in the field, it is never a guarantee that they will be approved at the hearings for many, possibly logistical reasons," Dente wrote in an email to HempBuild

Mag. "The committee expressed satisfaction with the diligence of the team and the fact checking we did and presented to them and it's the community's funding support that helps us do that work."

The approved changes for the first time incorporated fire-rated hemp-lime wall assemblies into the appendix, based on three ASTM E-119 one-hour fire tests. The tests were facilitated by Cameron McIntosh and conducted by Intertek Laboratories in York, PA in 2024 and 2025.

At the previous hearings in May in Orlando, FL, clarifications to include plaster when classifying a hemp-lime wall as a mass wall were approved. Mass walls have lower R-value requirements in most climate zones because the mass improves thermal performance.

Funding came from a crowdfunding campaign sponsored by HempBuild Magazine, Hemp Build School, and Americhanvre, which in one month raised $12,300 from about 40 donors. The funds covered the costs of code proposal preparation, attendance and testimony at ICC hearings, and related expenses.

"We are humbled and encouraged by the response to this fundraiser," McIntosh said.

Why the Code was Updated

The IRC covers one- and two-family dwellings, townhouses, and their accessory structures. It is updated every three years and serves as the model residential code for 49 states. (Wisconsin is the only exception).

Members of the International Residential Code Committee approve updates to Appendix BL unanimously 11-0 at the IRC Hearings in Cleveland, Oct. 23, 2025. Photo courtesy of Martin Hammer

However, adopting the appendices is voluntary. But already jurisdictions such as the City of Austin, TX and the state of Minnesota have adopted Appendix BL from the 2024 IRC for their 2026 residential code, giving a clear path for hemp-lime construction in those jurisdictions. Other jurisdictions, especially with advocacy, are likely to follow suit.

In jurisdictions where Appendix BL has not been adopted, the appendix can always be proposed to the local building official on a project basis. Its use is often granted because of the associated credibility of the IRC, and it is typically preferred to no guidance at all.

Even though hemp-lime has been proven fire-resistant in the EU for decades, US building departments are seeking confirmation, specifically through ASTM E119 and E84 tests, that hemp-lime is fire resistant. As wildfires and extreme climate events increase, the performance of mineral-based, highly fire-resistant materials such as hemp-lime is drawing more attention. And unlike petrochemical-derived insulation and foam products, hemp-lime produces no toxic gases if it burns.

"Fire is a rapidly increasing issue for building departments and everyone else," Tucson-based code co-author David Eisenberg told HempBuild Mag.

"Having evidence that these are better than conventional construction in terms of fire safety is a big issue." Having fire-rated wall assemblies in the codes will save time and money for hemp-lime builders and homeowners going forward when 1-hour walls are required, for example when a wall is less than 5 feet from a property line.

In Oregon, for example, hempcrete builder Karen Rugg of Perennial Building paid $8,000 for ASTM E-119 fire testing in 2022 to secure local approval for a single project. Under the new language, local jurisdictions will be able to rely on the rated assemblies included in the IRC, eliminating the need for costly project-specific testing.

Next Steps
With the IRC committee's approval, the proposed changes move into the Public Comment phase of the 2027 IRC code development this Spring. No public comment is expected for the Hemp-Lime appendix, which would mean the recently approved proposal would become part of Appendix BL in the 2027 IRC.

If included in the 2027 IRC, these additions to Appendix BL could significantly streamline permitting for hemp-lime builders nationwide—further integrating bio-based, fire-resistant, carbon-storing materials into mainstream construction.

LEADER PROFILE

ERIC MILBURN & TANNER BOWMAN
Hemp Was the Past, and Will be the Future.

Eric Milburn: I've loved hemp building since the moment I was introduced to it by my grandmother. I know that hemp is going to change the way we build homes. It will reduce the need for large HVAC systems, create healthy living environments, and become resilient structures that will last hundreds of years. **Tanner Bowman:** The Hemp industry interests me because of its inherent sustainability. The amount of carbon that hemp removes from the atmosphere may be crucial in the near future for creating a balanced environment. Hemp was the past, and will be the future.

EM: I first learned hemp building with the cast-in-place method but I see the industry shifting to the block method which saves on time and material. **TB:** I learned that although hempcrete does not have as much compression strength as normal concrete, it has greater shear strength.

What was a win for your company in the past year?

EM: Securing our first contract to build a hemp home in Colorado from start to finish. The best part is the design came from my Dad as the lead architect. **TB:** We have the opportunity to make this a very unique, sustainable, and beautiful house perched in the mountains of the front range.

Eric Milburn (L) and Tanner Bowman (R) are co-founders of Colorado-based Healthy Hemp Homes

What challenges does the hemp building industry face that it must overcome?

EM: The construction industry is built on decades of a "this is how we've always done it" mentality. We basically have to undo all of that while demonstrating to homeowners and builders that we can build a healthy, beautiful home without using harmful petroleum-based chemicals. **TB:** Hempcrete is unknown to a lot of people, and is unknown to a lot of the construction industry. I believe that this will change fast. Hempcrete and hemp products are going to be the new big hype, even surpassing electric cars.

GREEN BUILDERS/CONTRACTORS

AZ

DEVELOPMENT CENTER FOR APPROPRIATE TECHNOLOGY - *Tucson*
Contact: David Eisenberg
Decat.net

NEW EARTH DESIGN
- *Sedona*
Contact: Jeff Magus
Jeff@newearthdesign.us

OLD PUEBLO HEMP COMPANY - *Tucson*
Contact: Micaela Machado
Oldpueblohempco.com

CA

<u>Featured</u>
AARON GRAIL CONSTRUCTION
- *Sebastopol*
Contact: Aaron Grail
(707) 292 4097
Aarongrailconstruction.com
6400 Lone Pine Rd, Sebastopol, CA 95472
Aaron@aarongrailconstruction.com

<u>Featured</u>
RIVERDALE HEMP GIN
- *Riverdale*
Contact: Tom Pires
(918) 841-2289
Westernfibers.com/riverdale-gin
PO Box 366
RIVERDALE, CA, 93656
Develop@WesternFibers.com

BUCKEYE NATURAL BUILDERS
- *Scotts Valley*
Contact: Miles Taylor
Buckeyenaturalbuilders.com

CARBONL3SS MODULAR
- *Los Angeles*
Contact: Wilfredo Paz Bermudez, PE
Piecebypaz.us

DOTEK - *San Diego*
Contact: Chris Velsaco
Thedotek.com

FACTORY_OS - *Vallejo*
Contact: Rick Holliday
Factoryos.com

INDIGENOUS HABITAT INSTITUTE - *Trinidad*
Contact: Lisa Sundberg
Indigenoushabitatinstitute.com

OBSIDIAN GOLD
- *Fresno*
Contact: Elliot Bailey
Obsidiangold24@gmail.com

SOLSTICE ECO BUILDING - *Joshua Tree*
Contact: Nicholas Holmes
Solsticeeco.com

DYLAN TRIMARCHI
- *Bishop*
Dylantrimarchi@gmail.com

Hempcrete workshop at Complete Hemp Processing, Winfred, SD. Photo courtesy Jean Lotus

GREEN BUILDERS/CONTRACTORS

CO

Featured
HEALTHY HEMP HOMES
- Denver Metro
Contact: Eric Milburn
(970) 821-5461
Healthyhemphomes.org
855 Gray Street, Lakewood, CO 80214
Eric@healthyhemphomes.org

Featured
NATURALIA CONSTRUCTION *- Alamosa*
Contact: Gamal Jadue Zalaquette
Naturaliaconstruction.com
610 State Ave, Alamosa, CO 81101
Hello@naturaliaconstruction.com

Featured
HEMPIRE HOLDINGS CO
Contact: Sergiy Kovalenkov
+38 0676585350
Hempire.tech

Featured
EVOLVE CONSTRUCTION *- Steamboat Springs*
Contact: Jeremy Stephen
(970) 846-3178
Evolvehomebuild.com
PO Box 772536, Steamboat Springs, CO 80477
Jeremy@Evolvehomebuild.com

BAUEN BUILD *- Boulder*
Contact: Matt Brill
Bauenbuild.com

CORNERSTONE HOMES *- Lafayette*
Contact: Keenan Tompkins
Buildcornerstone.com

CITIZENS FOR CLEAN ENERGY *- Durango*
Contact: Steve Heising
Citizensforcleanenergy.org

EARTHEN ELEMENTS *- Paonia*
Contact: Dominic Anthony
Earthenelements.com

ELEVATED DESIGN BUILD *- Fort Collins*
Contact: David Kaplan
Elevateddesignbuild.com

HEMP HOGANS *- Paonia*
Contact: Nic Kola
Hemphogans.com

HIGH DESERT HEMP HOMES *- Howard*
Contact: Taylus Schley
Highdeserthemphomes.com

LIVING CRAFT DESIGN BUILD *- Arvada*
Contact: Frank Wetenkamp
Livingcraft.design

REZOLANA INSTITUTE *- San Luis*
Contact: Arnie Valdez
rezolana.av@gmail.com

PLASTER ARTISAN *- Paonia*
Contact: Kael Frank
Plasterartisan.com

ARTHUR WISEHART, BUILDER *- Paonia*
Contact: Arthur Wisehart
Wisehart@gmail.com

DE

Featured
HEMPBLOCK USA
-Lewes
Contact: Glen Donoghoe
(855) 760-0756
Hempblockusa.com
16192 Coastal Highway, Lewes, DE 19958
Admin@hempblockusa.com

Hempcrete home in Paonia, CO. Photo courtesy of Bronwen Barry.

GREEN BUILDERS/CONTRACTORS

Traci Quinn of Pink Hats Construction, packs hempcrete at a Chicago workshop. Photo courtesy Jean Lotus

FL
ATB SERVICES HEMP
- *Daytona Beach*
Contact: Robin Thoroughgood
Atbservicesllc.com

JONATHAN PORCELLI
- *St. Petersburg*
Jporcelli@mac.com

MATTAMY HOMES
- *Bradenton*
Contact: Jose Iturraspe
Jose.iturraspe@mattamycorp.com

ONX HOMES
- *Florida City*
Contact: Michael Marks
Onxhomes.com

HI
HEMP HOME HAWAII
- *Maui*
Contact: Joe Smith
Hemphomehawaii.com

PERMANENTLY AFFORDABLE LIVING KAUA'I - *Anahola*
Contact: Glen Head
Pal-kauai.org

IA
TIM WHITE, NATURAL BUILDER - *Waukon*
Contact: Tim White
Texashealthyhomes.com

ID
REGENERATIVE BUILDING SOLUTIONS
- *Driggs*
Contact: Lindsey Love
Regenbuilding.com

KY
PRESTON GREEN
- *Louisville*
Contact: Stephen Mercer
Prestongreen.net

IL
I GROW HOMES
- *Arcola*
Contact: Joshua Blackwell
Igrowhomes.com:

PINK HATS CONSTRUCTION & DEVELOPMENT
- *Chicago*
Contact: Traci Quinn
Pinkhatsconstructiondevgrp.com

LA
GRO ENTERPRISES
- *New Orleans*
Contact: Joel Holton
Groenterprises.biz

STRONG CONSTRUCTION - *Lafayette*
Contact: Joe Strong
Strong-construction.com

GREEN BUILDERS/CONTRACTORS

MA

Featured
HILLSIDE CENTER FOR SUSTAINABLE LIVING
Contact: David Hall
(978) 465-7047
Hillsidecenterforsustainable-living.com
2 Federal St., Newburyport, MA 01950
office@hallandmoskow.com

BAILEY DAVOL STUDIO BUILD - *Jamaica Plain*
Contact: Timothy Bailey
Studiobuildboston.com

BIOLITHIC BUILDS
- *Greater Boston*
Contact: Emily Wang
Biolithicbuilds@gmail.com

C.H. NEWTON BUILDERS, INC.
- *Falmouth*
Contact: Zachery Miller
Chnewton.com

HEMPSTONE LLC
- *Hatfield*
Contact: Tom Rossmassler
Hempstone.net

HOMEWORKS DESIGN BUILD - *Easthampton*
Contact: Lauren Faulkner Duncan
Homeworksdesignbuild.com

VALLEY HOUSING COOP
- *Connecticut River Valley*
Contact: Nevin Murray
Valleyhousing.coop

VILLAGE CARPENTRY AND LANDSCAPING
- *Goshen*
Contact: Shelby Howland
Villagecarpentryma.com

ME
LION CARPENTRY
- *Portland*
Contact: Ethan Lavendier
Mainelioncarpentry@gmail.com

MI
AURORA RENOVATES
- *Muskegon*
Contact: Brock Hyder
Aurorarenovates.com

BALECRAFT - *Traverse City*
Contact: Ellis Wills-Begley
Balecraft.com

A HempBLOCK workshop participant installs specially cut hempcrete blocks to fit around the steel frame. Photo courtesy of Crystal Cervantez-Tkac

GREEN BUILDERS/CONTRACTORS

Hempcrete-insulated Jellybeanz tire roundhouse in Fennville, MI. Photo courtesy of Airbnb

HEMP 4 HUMANITY
- *Detroit*
Contact: Cody Ley
H4h.earth

SUPER NATURAL STRUCTURES
- *Marquette*
Contact: Donald Samulski
Supernaturalstructures.com

WASHTENAW WOODWRIGHTS
- *Washtenaw*
Contact: Bruce Curtis
Woodwrights.com

MN
GOLDENROD STRUCTURES - *Minneapolis*
Contact: Dagan Bontrager
daganyb@gmail.com

LOWER SIOUX HEMP
- *Morton*
Contact: Danny Desjarlais
Lowersioux.com

MS
WILLISON TIMBERWORKS DESIGN BUILD, LLC - *Perkinston*
Contact: Seth Willison
Willisontimberworks.com

MT
BIG SKY HEMP - *Choteau*
Contact: Doug Weist
Farmtech.us

NC
BLUE RIDGE TINY HOMES - *Woodfin*
Contact: Greg Zocher
Blueridgetinyhomes.com

ND
Featured
HOMELAND HEMPCRETE
Contact: Matthew Marino
Homelandhempco.com
(701) 426-3796
551 Airport Rd, Bismarck, ND 58504
Matt@homelandhempco.com

GRASSROOTS DEVELOPMENT - *Fargo*
Contact: Justin Berg
Grassrootsdev.co

NE
GENERAL HEMPCONSTRUCTION - *Denton*
Contact: Tina Jones
Generalhempconstruction@outlook.com

NM
B. PUBLIC PREFAB
- *Santa Fe*
Contact: Mariana Pickering
Bpublicprefab.com

REFUGE INDUSTRIAL HEMP BUILDING
- *Albuquerque*
Contact: Robin Elkin
Refugehempnm@gmail.com

GREEN BUILDERS/CONTRACTORS

ST. FRANCIS HOMELESSNESS CHALLENGE - *Taos*
Contact: Amy Farah Weiss
Saintfrancischallenge.org

NY

HARMONY BUILDERS - *Woodstock*
Contact: Michael Hicks
Harmonybuilders.com

WILLIAM T. HUGO - *Amagansett*
Wmhugo@aol.com

LATITUDE REGENERATIVE REAL ESTATE - *Kingston*
Contact: David Todd
Chooselatitude.com/david-todd

REGENERATIVE PATHWAYS - *Canaan*
Contact: Nick Salmons
Regenerativepathways.com

RONDOUT NATURAL BUILDERS - *Kingston*
Contact: Jeff Gagnon
Rondoutnaturalbuilders@gmail.com

TURNER CONSTRUCTION - *NYC*
Contact: Joel Ahearne-Ray
Turnerconstruction.com

WOODSTOCK HEMPCRETE - *Woodstock*
Contact: Paul Petrov
Woodstockhempcrete.com

OH

NEW HOME PARTNER - *Columbus*
Contact: Jason Heidenescher
Newhomepartner@gmail.com

URBAN GREEN DESIGN - *Cincinnati*
Contact: Jeremy Schlicher
Urbangreendesignltd.com

OK

HIWASSEE HEALTHY HOMES - *Arcadia*
Contact: Cory Davis
Hiwasseehealthyhomes.com

OR

ADAM ALFONSO - *Salem*
Adam.m.alfonso@gmail.com

DOMESTIC TRANQUILITY - *Eugene*
Contact: Win Swafford
Resilienteugene.com

ECONEST BUILDING CO. - *Ashland*
Contact: Robert LaPorte
Econesthomes.com

FAMILY 1ST BUILDING & REMODELING - *La Pine*
Contact: Diana Forsberg
Family1stbr.com

HEMPTOWN ON MAIN - *Jacksonville*
Contact: Greg Flavell
Hemptownonmain.org

PERENNIAL BUILDING, LLC - *Sisters*
Contact: Karen Rugg
Perennialbuilding.com

SHELTER WORKS LTD. - *Philomath*
Contact: Thomas VanDenend
Healthyshelterworks.com

Hillsboro, West Virginia hempcrete home. Photo courtesy of Seven Rivers Design Build.

GREEN BUILDERS/CONTRACTORS

PA

COEXIST BUILD
- Blandon
Contact: Anastasiya Konopitskaya
Coexist.build

DEEP SPRING TIMBERFRAMES, LLC - *Pittsburgh*
Contact: Jiri Vrsek
Deepspringframes.com

RI

CH NEWTON - *Newport*
Contact: Zachery Miller
Chnewton.com

TN

AERA - *Nashville*
Contact: Taylor LaForge
Aerasystems.co

TX

`Featured`
HEMP BUILD NETWORK
Contact: Ray Kaderli
(540) 664-6499
New Braunfels, TX

DEL TORO NATURAL BUILDERS - *Mason*
Contact: Darren Del Toro
Deltoronaturalbuilders.com

FLOURISH HERE
- Dripping Springs
Contact: Noralinda Ureste
Flourishhere.com

GRADEK CONTRACTING AND DESIGNS
Contact: Carl Gradek
Gradekcontracting.com

TEXAS COB CO
- Kingsbury
Contact: Simon Gonzalez
Texascob.com

Hempcrete ADU in Austin TX with legacy oak trees.
Photo courtesy of Carl Gradek

GREEN BUILDERS/CONTRACTORS

Hempcrete home and community center (9,000 sq. ft), Asheville, NC. Photo courtesy Tim Callahan

VA
RBW DESIGN BUILD
- *Virginia Beach*
Contact: Robert Bridges
Rbwdesignbuild.com

VT
NEW FRAMEWORKS
- *Essex Junction*
Contact: Ace McArleton
Newframeworks.com

WA
Featured
NEXT GENESIS DESIGN
- *White Salmon*
Contact: John Hutton
(312) 339-8248
Nextgenesisdesign.com
8 Debo Road, White Salmon, WA 98672
John@Nextgenesisdesign.com

HAPPY HEALTHY HOME
- *Salmon*
Contact: Yaniv Koby
Happyhealthyhomenw.com

LIMELIFE CONSTRUCTION - *Chehalis*
Contact: Andrew Hancock
Drew.hancock@sbcglobal.net

NATURAL ECO BUILDERS - *Seattle*
Contact: Terrance Aaron Lee-Hammond
Naturalecobuilders@gmail.com

NORTHWEST HEMP BUILDERS
Contact: Matt Eckland
Nwhempbuilders@gmail.com

STEENPAD
- *Bainbridge Island*
Contact: Klaas Hesselink
Steenpad.com

WI
HIGHLAND INDUSTRIAL HEMP - *Watertown*
Contact: Todd Strauss
Highlandindustrialhemp.com

Featured
SATIVA BUILDING SYSTEMS
Contact: Zachery Popp
(715) 470-0677
Sativabuildingsystems.com
N6416 Banner Road
Wittenberg, WI 54499
Zach@sativapanel.com

WV
SEVEN RIVERS DESIGN BUILD - *Hillsboro*
Contact: Andrew Must
Sevenriversdesignbuild.com

LEADER PROFILE

JEREMY STEPHEN
US Hemp Hurd Supply Chain can Now Keep up with Demand

I founded Evolve Construction, LLC and began contracting in 2007. Since 2017, I have solely focused on hempcrete structures, supply chains, and permitted structures. I was one of the first in Colorado to get a hempcrete Certificate of Occupancy in Steamboat Springs. My company continues to innovate more affordable ways to build with hempcrete in conjunction with traditional methods and hempcrete blocks where suited. Industrial hemp construction is a path to healthy, sustainable, efficient, safe and affordable housing.

What was a win for your company in the past year? Under budget and ahead of schedule, we are building a custom 3,200 sq ft hempcrete panel home in Hotchkiss, CO to be completed in April 2026.

Jeremy R. Stephen is general contractor and owner of Evolve Construction, based in Steamboat Springs, CO

What is something about hemp building/construction/processing you didn't know a year ago?

Hemp seed sorting is creating standardization and we now have a US-based hemp hurd supply chain that can keep up with our demand.

What bottlenecks have you observed in the industrial hemp industry and how would you solve them?

It's important to get life-long industry experts involved, starting at the hemp seed, in order to achieve higher quality and standardization of raw materials and availability for hempcrete/hemplime construction.

> *Industrial hemp construction is a path to healthy, sustainable, efficient, safe and affordable housing.*

HEMP BUILDING DIRECTORY 2026

LEADER PROFILE

AARON GRAIL
Hempcrete and Bio-Based Building Systems are the Future of High Performance Building

We specialize in high-performance building, using advanced systems and carbon-capturing materials to create sustainable, healthier homes. Unlike traditional systems with 10+ components, hemp construction uses just three, ensuring ease of assembly without sacrificing reliability or efficiency. It's an elegant, effective and sustainable solution.

What was a win for your company in the past year?

A big win for my company this past year was moving from advocacy into real traction.
We didn't just talk about healthier, low-carbon building—we actually got projects permitted, built, and taken seriously by officials and architects.

Hempcrete is a system, not a product. When it's treated like insulation or structure or finish in isolation, projects struggle. When it's treated like a wall system with specific boundaries, everything clicks.
In California, the primary barrier facing hemp and other bio-based and earthen building materials is regulatory lock-in created by Assembly Bill (AB) 130.

AB 130 froze most changes to the California Residential Code through 2031 to reduce permitting barriers, but in doing so, unintentionally blocked recognition of proven, fire-resistive, and cost-effective materials already recognized in the International Residential Code, including hemp-lime. The Department of Housing and Community Development declined to consider IRC appendices for these materials without legislative direction. Californians rebuilding in wildfire-prone areas are denied safer, lower-carbon options, and builders face unnecessary permitting friction. We are petitioning the Legislature to amend AB 130 to allow voluntary use and ensure proper guidance for the application of these systems.

Aaron Grail is owner of Aaron Grail Construction, based in Sebastopol, CA.

Considering a custom hempcrete home?

We have expert advice.

From start-to-finish, we can take care of design, permitting, engineering, construction, insurance, and Certificates of Occupancy!

Established in 2007, Evolve Construction has a proven track record in hempcrete construction; completing multiple projects in various counties across Colorado.

Our Services Include:
- Ground-up design & build services
- On-site & prefab systems
- Year-round hempcrete construction
- Free hempcrete consultations
- Builder training & workshops
- Building permit fast-tracking / liaison services
- Hempcrete materials evaluation

BUILDING SUSTAINABLE + HEALTHY HOMES
evolvecobuild.com
info@evolvecobuild.com
970-846-3178

EVOLVE CONSTRUCTION

Nationwide

HEMP BUILDING COMPANY

Services & Materials

CONSTRUCTION
Hemplime Block installation
New Builds & Retrofits
Cast In-Situ

TRAINING
Workshops
Onsite Training
Worksite Safety & Organization
Installer Certification

MATERIALS
Hemplime Blocks
Building Grade Hemp Hurd
Lime Binders
Minerals & Additives
Lime & Clay Plasters

PLASTERING
Interior and Exterior
Finish Plasters

info@hempbuildingco.com

1.720.231.6865

www.hempbuildingco.com

@hempbuildingcompany

LEADER PROFILE

DAVID HALL
Hemp Building is Simple and Eliminates Construction Waste

The simplicity of hemp building interests me most, because construction uses fewer tapes, adhesives and membranes and generates so much less waste.

What was a win for your company in the past year?

The very quick lease up of all 12 units in our hempcrete multifamily development at the Hillside Center for Sustainable Living in Newburyport.

What bottlenecks have you observed in the industrial hemp industry and how would you solve them?

The bottleneck for hemp construction regionally is the absence of affordable, delivered, dust free, consistent, USA-grown hemp fiber here in Northern New England.

David D. Hall is partner at Hillside Center for Sustainable Living and Moskow/Linn Architects based in Newburyport, MA.

Multiunit hempcrete tip-up units at Hillside Center for Sustainable Living, Newburyport, MA. Photo courtesy of Hall & Moskow, Newburyport, MA.

HEMP BUILDING DIRECTORY 2026

LEADER PROFILE

PHELAN DALTON
Hemp Homes Exceed Performance Expectations

I am intrigued by hemp-lime's versatility in building, its forgiving nature, and easy repairability. We build homes in harsh climates above 5000' elevation and fire-danger zones. Our clients report that their homes' performance exceeds expectations. I continue to be fascinated by hemp-lime's thermal and hygroscopic capabilities.

This year we completed our first full Hemplime Block build in Santa Fe New Mexico. We also supplied blocks to a few other builders who completed other Hemplime Block projects as well.

What bottlenecks have you observed in the natural building industry and how would you solve them?

It all starts with the farmers and processors. If the USA could implement secondary processing to market the fiber, processors wouldn't have to rely so much on the hurd for revenue and the price for US grown hurd could hopefully come down.

Phelan Dalton is CEO of Colorado-based The Hemp Building Company in charge of project management, material distribution and client consultations.

> " *I am intrigued by hemp-lime's versatility in building, its forgiving nature, and easy repairability.* "

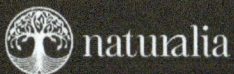

Naturalia Construction

We specialize in hemp homes and commercial buildings, combining durability, energy efficiency, and sustainability with spaces that support a healthier future.

Our Services

- 🏠 Hemp Building
- ❀ Hemp Remodeling
- 🌱 Hemplime Material Supplies
- ☀ Solar Energy
- 🚽 Septic System
- 💧 Well Installation

We don't just build, we also train contractors and crews in professional hempcrete construction.

CALL US TODAY!

📞 +1 (732) 239-3758   🌐 www.naturaliaconstruction.com

GREEN LIVING IN NEWBURYPORT

1, 2, & 3+ Bedroom Residences Available for Lease
HillsideSustainableLiving.com

PRIVATE OUTDOOR SPACE
Expand your living space to private rooftop terraces, patios, and covered farmers porches.

SOLAR POWERED
Kill your electric bill and power your entire home with solar energy produced on your roof.

SHARED ELECTRIC TRANSPORTATION
Can your second car by driving community Smart Cars and living walking distance to the Boston Commuter Rail and Downtown Newburyport.

COMMUNITY AMENITIES
Access co-working space, guest suites and an outdoor, kitchen, terrace, and fireplace outside your doorstep.

ENERGY EFFICIENT HOUSING
Make a radical reduction in your heating and cooling needs.

FOOD AND FARMING
Eat food grown in your backyard year-round.

Largest US commercial hempcrete project underway at
HILLSIDE CENTER FOR SUSTAINABLE LIVING
Newburyport, MA • (978) 502-1868
hillsidecenterforsustainableliving.com

LEADER PROFILE

SERGIY KOVALENKOV
Hemp Building is Beneficial for the Society and the Environment

This year, I've observed how hemp-lime performs in different climates from extremely cold places like Canada to tropical climates like Thailand. I like to see how different varieties of hemp are cultivated in different climates.

What was a win for your company in the past year?

Hempire has started to supply materials and execute projects in Thailand. We are happy to expand to the Asian market. Also, We have started to supply our binders to the largest commercial project in the United States - Kosmos Stargazing Resort in Colorado.

What is something about hemp building/construction/processing you didn't know a year ago?

You have to be extremely careful about using this material in a tropical climate. A thick layer of dense hemp-lime, lack of sun, lack of ventilation and high humidity can help mold show up on the surface of the hemp-lime wall.

Sergiy "Doctor Hemphouse" Kovalenkov is the founder of Hempire, based in Ukraine and Colorado, USA.

What bottlenecks or challenges have you observed in the industrial hemp industry and how would you solve them?

We have a lack of funding and government support for farmers to start serious cultivation and processing operations. There is also a lack of awareness and ignorance from architects and government officials, which slows down the expansion of the hemp building sector. This sector needs environmentally conscious investors, who are willing to go "all-in" and become part of something really big and beneficial for the society and the environment. More educational programs must be implemented on all levels to breed new kinds of architects and builders.

> " *This year, I've observed how hemp-lime performs in different climates from extremely cold places like Canada to tropical climates like Thailand.* "

LEADER PROFILE

JOHN HUTTON
Hemp-Lime Provides an Inspiring Way to Build

With over 20 years of experience focused on natural building technologies, I provide the knowledge, skills, and coordination required to design, engineer, permit, and construct buildings using natural materials such as hemp-lime.

What draws me to hemp-lime construction is its ability to address one of the most significant and least acknowledged crises in the built environment today: the widespread toxicity of conventional building materials.

From formaldehyde-based glues in particle board to heavy metals in gypsum wallboard, PFAS in house wraps, and VOCs such as benzene, ammonia, and formaldehyde in paints, the materials used in most modern homes contain carcinogens, endocrine disruptors, and respiratory irritants.

Hemp-lime offers a fundamentally different paradigm. It is completely non-toxic, vapor-open, and chemically stable. It regulates moisture, buffers indoor humidity, and is exceptionally resistant to mold, pests, and fire. Its combination of thermal mass and insulation creates a remarkably stable, clean, and comfortable indoor environment that supports human well-being rather than undermining it.

John Hutton is founder and principal designer at Next Genesis Design, based in White Salmon, WA

For me, the most inspiring aspect of hemp-lime is that it provides a way to build that is healthier for people, healthier for the environment, and more aligned with the craft and integrity of good construction.

What was a win for your company in the past year?

• Winning the 2025 USHBA Hempcrete Building of the Year award.
• Completion of the largest hemp-lime building on the West Coast in collaboration with Rijka Timberframes
• Design, engineering, permitting and construction coordination of 5 hemp-lime homes, located in 5 different building jurisdictions.
• Training upwards of 100 students in the installation of hemp-lime and natural plasters.

HEMP BUILDING CONSULTANTS

Hempcrete duplex on Lower Sioux Reservation, Morton, MN. Photo courtesy of Jean Lotus

CO
Featured
HEMP BUILDING COMPANY
- Lafayette
Contact: Phelan Dalton
Info@hempbuildingco.com
Hempbuildingco.com
(720) 231-6865

Featured
HEMPIRE HOLDINGS CO
Hempire.tech
Contact: Sergiy Kovalenkov
+38 0676585350

DE
Featured
HEMPBLOCK USA
Hempblockusa.com
Contact: Glen Donoghoe
Admin@hempblockusa.com
16192 Coastal Highway,
Lewes, DE 19958
(855) 760-0756

ID
Featured
HEMPITECTURE, INC.
421 E 500 S #100,
Jerome, ID 83338
Contact: Mattie Mead
mattie@hempitecture.com
(208) 218-8698
Hempitecture.com

PA
Featured
AMERICHANVRE CAST HEMP
Contact: Cameron McIntosh
(833) 443-6727
Americhanvre.com
1529 Brookside Road,
Allentown, PA 18106
cameron@americhanvre.com

TX
Featured
HEMP BUILD NETWORK
New Braunfels, TX
Contact: Ray Kaderli
(540) 664-6499

crownjade

Build smart. Build green. Build with confidence.

READY TO BUILD WITH HEMP-LIME (HEMPCRETE) OR OTHER BIO-BASED SYSTEMS?

Crown Jade Design & Engineering provides:
• Permit-ready architectural & structural sets
• Plans tailored for hemp-lime, rammed earth, straw-bale & other sustainable materials
• Local Colorado expertise with national alternatives experience

crownjade.com | (970) 472-2394| Greeley CO

HEMP ARCHITECTS/DESIGNERS

Hempcrete Roundhouse, Nevada Co., CA. Photo courtesy of Jonny BambooTao

AZ

ALEXANDER SEXSMITH ARCHITECTS - *Tucson*
Contact: Alex Sexsmith
Asxsmith@gmail.com

DEVELOPMENT CENTER FOR APPROPRIATE TECHNOLOGY
- *Tucson*
Contact: David Eisenberg
Dcat.net

NEW EARTH DESIGN
- *Sedona*
Contact: Jeff Magus
Jeff@newearthdesign.us

URBAN RURAL & DESIGN STUDIO
- *Flagstaff*
Contact : BriAnn Laban
Urdstudio.com

CA

ARCHITECTURAL RESOURCE CONSULTANTS - *Tustin*
Contact: John Russo
Arc-corporate.com

ARKIN TILT ARCHITECTS
- *Berkeley*
Contact: Anni Tilt
Arkintilt.com

BRIGHTWORKS SUSTAINABILITY NETWORK - *Oakland*
Contact: Heath Blount
Brightworks.net

BUILDERS WITHOUT BORDERS, INC.
- *Berkeley*
Contact: Martin Hammer
Builderswithoutborders.org

GAVIN FRASER ARCHITECT
- *San Francisco*
Contact: Gavin Fraser
Gavinfraser.com

HIGH SIERRA ARCHITECTURE
- *Mammoth Lakes*
Contact: Nathaniel Taylor
Highsierraarchitecture.com

MBH ARCHITECTS
- *Alameda*
Contact: John McNulty
Mbharch.com

MILLIØNS - *Los Angeles*
Contact: John May
Millionsarchitecture.com

STARSEED CREATIVE
- *Nevada City*
Contact: Neil Decker
Starseedcreative.com

HEMP ARCHITECTS/DESIGNERS

CO
Featured
CROWN JADE DESIGN & ENGINEERING - *Greeley*
Contact: Mark Benjamin
(970) 472-2394
Crownjade.com
PO Box 336702 Greeley, CO, 80633
Mark@crownjade.com

Featured
HEALTHY HEMP HOMES
- *Denver Metro*
Contact: David Milburn
(970) 821-5461
Healthyhemphomes.org
855 Gray Street, Lakewood, CO 80214
David@healthyhemphomes.org

Featured
NATURALIA CONSTRUCTION
- *Alamosa*
Contact: Gamal Jadue Zalaquette
Naturaliaconstruction.com
610 State Ave, Alamosa, CO 81101
Hello@naturaliaconstruction.com

ADAMAH DESIGN
- *La Veta*
Contact: Aliyah Field
Adamahdesign.com

CRANSBURY DESIGN
- *Paonia*
Contact: Christina Ransbury
Cransbury.com

DF SWOBODA ARCHITECTURE
- *Boulder*
Contact: David Swoboda
Dfswoboda.com

ELEVATED DESIGN BUILD - *Fort Collins*
Contact: David Kaplan
Elevateddesignbuild.com

LIVING CRAFT DESIGN BUILD - *Arvada*
Contact: Frank Wetenkamp
Livingcraft.design

LAND AND WATER CONCEPTS - *Salida*
Contact: Andy Riemenschneider
Andy@lwconcepts.com

RODWIN ARCHITECTURE - *Boulder*
Contact: Scott Rodwin
Rodwinarch.com

SIMA ARCHITECTURE & DESIGN LLC - *Denver*
Contact: Crystal Cervantez-Tkac
Simadesign.us

ARNIE VALDEZ
- *San Luis*
Certified.naturallygrown.org

DE
Featured
HEMPBLOCK USA
Contact: Glen Donoghoe
(855) 760-0756
Hempblockusa.com
16192 Coastal Highway, Lewes, DE 19958
Admin@hempblockusa.com

ID
REGENERATIVE BUILDING SOLUTIONS
- *Driggs*
Contact: Lindsey Love
Regenbuilding.com

Hempcrete home in LaVeta CO. Photo courtesy Jean Lotus

HEMP ARCHITECTS/DESIGNERS

Hempcrete addition in Rolling Hills, CA, installed in 2015. Photo courtesy of Beate Kirmse.

MA

Featured

HILLSIDE CENTER FOR SUSTAINABLE LIVING
Contact: David Hall
(978) 465-7047
Hillsidecenterforsustainable-living.com
2 Federal St., Newburyport, MA 01950
Office@hallandmoskow.com

ARCHITECTURE TOWARDS NEUTRAL
- *Dorchester*
Contact: Sara Kudra
Archtowards.com

CAMBRIDGE SEVEN
- *Cambridge*
Contact: Jacob Bloom
Cambridgeseven.com

COEVERYTHING
- *Somerville*
Contact: Miriam Gee
Coeverything.co

HOMEWORKS DESIGN BUILD - *Easthampton*
Contact: Lauren Faulkner-Duncan
Homeworksdesignbuild.com

JOHNSON ROBERTS ASSOCIATES ARCHITECTS
- *Somerville*
Contact: Natalie Eringos
Johnson-roberts.com

KENNEDY & VIOLICH ARCHITECTURE - *Boston*
Contact: Katie Koskey
Kvarch.net

MASS DESIGN GROUP
- *Boston*
Contact: James Kitchin, Franciso Colom
Massdesigngroup.org

NEXT PHASE STUDIOS ARCHITECTS
- *Brookline*
Contact: Lisa Sun, Florence MA
Nps-architects.com

BAILEY DAVOL/STUDIO BUILD - *Jamaica Plain*
Contact: Tim Bailey
Bd-sb.net

KIKO THÉBAUD ARCHITECTS
- *Greater Boston*
Contact: Kiko Thébaud
Kikothebaud@gmail.com

MD

PASSIVE TO POSITIVE ARCHITECTURE
- *Baltimore*
Contact: Michael Hindle
Passivetopositive.com

MI

BALECRAFT
- *Traverse City*
Contact: Ellis Wills-Begley
Balecraft.com

HEMP ARCHITECTS/DESIGNERS

MN

A + WORKS CONSULTING
- *Minneapolis*
Contact: Anna Koosmann
Akoosmann@gmail.com

ALM DESIGN STUDIO
- *Minneapolis*
Contact: Lucas Alm
Almdesignstudio.com

MSR DESIGN
- *Minneapolis*
Contact: Simona Fisher AIA
Msrdesign.com

OERTAL ARCHITECTS
- *Minneapolis*
Contact: Janneke Schaap
Oertelarchitects.com

MS

WILLISON TIMBERWORKS DESIGN BUILD, LLC - *Perkinston*
Contact: Seth Willison
Willisontimberworks.com

MT

COLLIER CONCEPTS
- *Whitefish*
Contact: Kim Collier
Collierconcpets.com

LOVE/SCHACK ARCHITECTURE
- *Bozeman*
Contact: Lindsey Schack
Loveschackarchitecture.com

MASS DESIGN GROUP
- *Bozeman*
Contact: James Kitchin
Massdesigngroup.org

NC

CALLAHAN HOME DESIGNS - *Asheville*
Contact: Tim Callahan
T.l.callahan@icloud.com

WHAT ON EARTH ARCHITECTURE - *Asheville*
Contact: Jonathan Lucas
Whatoneartharchitecture.com

ND

`Featured`
HOMELAND HEMPCRETE
Contact: Matthew Marino
(701) 426-3796
Homelandhempco.com
551 Airport Rd, Bismarck, ND 58504
Matt@homelandhempco.com

NM

NATHANIEL CORUM, AIA
- *Santa Fe*
Massdesigngroup.org

NY

A SPACE UNFOLDS - *NYC*
Contact: Ines Yupanqui
Aspaceunfolds.com

CHRISTINA GRIFFIN STUDIOS - *Hastings on Hudson*
Contact: Christina Griffin
Christinagriffinarchitect.com

HEALTHY AFFORDABLE MATERIALS PROJECT
- *NYC*
Contact: Alison Mears
Healthymaterialshealthyhomes.org

JANUS WELTON DESIGN WORKS - *Woodstock*
Contact: Janus Welton
Janusweltondesignworks.com

MAGNUSSON ARCHITECTURE AND PLANNING PC - *NYC*
Contact: Sara Bayer
Maparchitects.com

SKYE RUOZZI - *Brooklyn*
skyeruozzi.com

TURNER CONSTRUCTION
- *NYC*
Contact: Joel Ahearne-Ray
Turnerconstruction.com

Hempcrete villa at Kosmos Stargazing Resort, Mosca, CO. Photo courtesy of Jean Lotus

HEMP ARCHITECTS/DESIGNERS

YOUARETHECITY
- *Brooklyn*
Contact: Kaja Kühl
Youarethecity.com

OH
URBAN GREEN DESIGN - *Cincinnati*
Contact: Jeremy Schlicher
Urbangreendesignltd.com

OR
DAY ONE DESIGN
- *Eugene*
Contact: Erica Bush
Dayonedesign.org

CONVERGENCE ARCHITECTURE
- *Portland*
Contact: Adam Robins
Convergencearch.com

ECONEST ARCHITECTURE
- *Ashland*
Contact: Paula Baker-Laporte
Econestarchitecture.com

HEMP TECHNOLOGIES GLOBAL - *Jacksonville*
Contact: Greg Flavall
Hemptechglobal.com

PA
COEXIST BUILD, LLC
- *Blandon*
Contact: Ana Konopitskaya
Coexist.build

GREEN BUILDING ALLIANCE - *Pittsburgh*
Contact: Jenna Cramer
Gba.org

RI
ESTES TWOMBLEY + TITRINGTON ARCHITECTS - *Newport*
Contact: Adam Titrington
Ettarchitects.com

WETHERBEE ARCHITECTS
- *Tiverton*
Contact: Emily Wetherbee
Wetherbee.com

SC
Featured
ROOTDOWN DESIGNS
- *Charleston*
Contact: April Magill
PO Box 13945, Charleston, SC 29412
Rootdowndesigns.com
Info@rootdowndesigns.com
(843) 252-0151

TN
HAVEN EARTH, PMA
- *Old Fort*
Contact: Paul River Richardson
Havenearth.biz

TX
BIOBUILD STUDIO
- *Austin*
Contact: Caroline Dunn
Biobuild.studio

MELL LAWRENCE ARCHITECTS - *Austin*
Contact: Mell Lawrence
Melllawrencearchitects.com

HEMP ARCHITECTS/DESIGNERS

PERKINS+WILL - *Austin*
Contact: Kendall Clauss
Perkinswill.com/studio/austin

PLURAL OFFICE ARCHITECTS, LLC
Contact: Joshua Carel
Pluraloffice.com

STEWARDSHIP INC.
- *Austin*
Contact: Gail Borst
Stewardshiparchitecture.com

VA

DRAWING CONCLUSIONS, LLC
- *Alexandria*
Contact: Valerie Amor, LEED AP, CPHD, CC-P
Valeriejamor@gmail.com

VT

ESCHER DESIGN INC.
- *Dorset*
Contact: Bob Escher
Escherdesigninc.com

NEW FRAMEWORKS
- *Essex Junction*
Contact: Ace McArleton
Newframeworks.com

VERMONT INTEGRATED ARCHITECTURE
- *Middlebury*
Contact: Megan Nedzinski
Vermontintegratedarchitecture.com

WA

Featured
NEXT GENESIS DESIGN
- *White Salmon*
Nextgenesisdesign.com
Contact: John Hutton
(312) 339-8248
8 Debo Road, White Salmon, WA 98672
john@nextgenesisdesign.com

A GREENER SPACE
- *Spokane*
Contact: Anjanette Green
agreenerspace.com

DEBORAH TODD BUILDING DESIGN SERVICES - *Bellingham*
Contact: Deborah Todd
Dtbuildingdesign.com

HAPPY HEALTHY HOME
- *Salmon*
Contact: Yaniv Koby
Happyhealthyhomenw.com

MILLER HULL - *Seattle*
Contact: Michael Hemer, AIA
millerhull.com

Howard, CO hempcrete home. Photo courtesy The Hemp Building Company

HEMP BUILDING DIRECTORY 2026

LEADER PROFILE

APRIL MAGILL

Renewable, Biogenic, Anti-Fungal, Hygroscopic Properties make Hempcrete Intriguing

Hempcrete's ability to work well with conventional construction, its low embodied carbon, renewable and biogenic, and its anti-fungal/anti-mold hygroscopic properties all make hempcrete and hemp-based construction materials intriguing.

What was a win for your company in the past year?

Our non-profit organization was awarded a federal EPA Community Change grant to be the architectural lead on a project to address healthy and affordable housing in a disadvantaged community in Charleston, SC.

We are also proud of our continued advancement of our hempcrete house plans (Hempsteads), being the co-keynote speaker at the West Coast Natural Building Conference (CASBA), and the completion of our hempcrete pilot project construction. This year, I am getting familiar with the recently adopted IRC building code for hemp-lime construction.

What bottlenecks have you observed in the industrial hemp industry and how would you solve them?

We need more qualified builders who understand hemp-lime construction; we are working to help educate and provide building workshops as well as a pilot project which will track performance over time. We need easily-accessible, high quality house plans for hemp-lime homes; we have provided these through Root Down House Plan Co. and will continue to build those resources.

April Magill is owner & principal architect at Charleston, SC-based Root Down Designs and Root Down House Plan Co. She is also founder of non-profit Root Down Building Collective

> " *We need more qualified builders who understand hemp-lime construction* "

VERDANT
Structural Engineers

Verdant Structural Engineers (VSE) is a full-service design firm providing structural drawings and calculations required for building permit submittal, product development, and research. VSE works on a large variety of projects ranging from residential to mid-rise mixed-use commercial construction.

LICENSED ACROSS THE USA, LOCATED IN BERKELEY, CA

INDUSTRY LEADER IN ALTERNATIVE BUILDING MATERIALS

ENGINEER ALL-NATURAL & LOW CARBON STRUCTURAL SYSTEMS

LEAD ENGINEER FOR HEMP INTERNATIONAL RESIDENTIAL CODE APPENDIX

• HEMPCRETE •
ADOBE • STRAW BALE • COB • EARTHBAG • RAMMED EARTH

2025 AWARD OF MERIT AT
GREEN HOME + DESIGN AWARDS IN MAINE

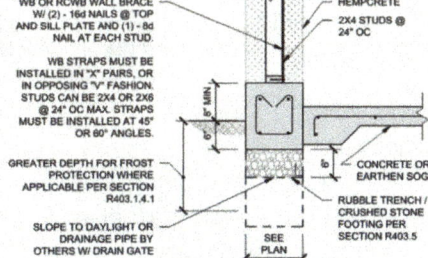

PHOTOS BY: ETHAN LAVENDIER
PHOTO BY: HARRY (HEMPHOMES.COM)

CONTACT   verdantstructural.com | admin@verdantstructural.com

LEADER PROFILE

ANTHONY DENTE
Simplifying Systems to Scale Natural Materials

I handle project acquisition and management, outreach and marketing and company vision and steering. I also manage our unique panelized straw product that was developed with the support of the EPA.

Carbon-storing and non-toxic materials will be the building materials of the future. I have a strong interest in doing what I can with my skillset and resources to help facilitate the switch to these materials as an industry and culture.

What was a win for your company in the past year?

We are still experiencing a significant increase in demand for engineering services pertaining to low-carbon, deep-green, carbon-storing, and natural building systems across the US. We are also receiving more inquiries from product developers who are trying to simplify these types of systems so that they can scale more easily.

This year, I learned a lot more about the complications of the PCR and EPD development process for hemp and other biogenic products and materials. It will be a long haul and needs support.

What bottlenecks have you observed in the industrial hemp industry and how would you solve them?

The biggest problems I see facing the hemp community from my lens are 1) developing a better process and/or testing for lateral load system selection or lateral load resistance in high seismic zones, 2) more clarity and understanding around hempcrete's actual embodied carbon value with the lime binder but also the lime plasters properly accounted for and 3) a better understanding of possible expansion of allowable finishes, beyond plaster, that do not conflict with moisture protection.

Anthony Dente is CEO of Berkeley, CA-based Verdant Structural Engineers and Verdant Building Products.

> *Carbon-storing and non-toxic materials will be the building materials of the future.*

MICAELA MACHADO
Nature Provides All that We Need

My husband and I are the proud owners of Old Pueblo Hemp Co in Tucson, AZ. I am the qualifying party for our General Contracting Services and Professional Hemp Cheerleader.

I feel grounded with hemp and bio-construction. It makes me feel like a human. Like I'm doing what I should be doing while I'm here on the planet for this short time. It makes me feel like I'm part of the Earth and connected to the past. I love that nature provides all that we need and it's shocking how far we've come from recognizing that.

What was a win for your company in the past year?
This past year we completed a most awesome project at an educational sleep away camp called Camp Cooper here in Tucson. We made over 16,000 hemp blocks, wrapped six existing cabins with our blocks from the exterior and then plastered the cabins. The cabin renovations turned out so beautifully and now for the rest of Camp Cooper's existence, these kids will experience hemp and learn about the whole process when they stay in their magical hemp cabins. They don't know how lucky they are!

Micaela Machado is co-owner of Old Pueblo Hemp Company, based in Tucson, AZ

Only very recently have I gotten to experience growing hemp from seed. We're doing the whole harvesting and retting process (chinanpa style!) and soon we will separate the fibers from hurd and spin the fiber. All on a very very small scale but it has really taught me even more appreciation and respect for this plant and how incredibly powerful it is in our hands. A local farmer is creating a desert-adapted variety before my very eyes and it is super inspiring.

> " *I love that nature provides all that we need and it's shocking how far we've come from recognizing that.* "

LEADER PROFILE

MARK BENJAMIN
Bioconstruction is Simplicity, Ease and Solid Construction

I run CJDE and run the engineering calcs for most of our jobs. I redline the plans for my drafters to prepare.

I taught myself strawbale engineering back before I started CJDE in 2004. My first hemp-lime hand-packed job was in 2014, and I've been active since then. I am doing six this year so far, including the Kosmos Stargazing community. My sons built the first house in Colorado when I moved here in 1994. I told them there are a million pieces of wood, with a million nails, in a conventional home. I like the simplicity, ease, and solid construction in hemp and all bioconstruction.

Mark Benjamin is president & principal engineer of Greeley, CO-based Crown Jade Design & Engineering.

pressed with how sturdy they are for shear value. I use the compressive value of the material for resisting shear loads.

What bottlenecks have you observed in the industrial hemp industry and how would you solve them?

The biggest obstacle, as I've been in construction my whole life before becoming an engineer, is changing the construction industry's outlook. I've seen it in my construction career, and now in my design/engineering career.

What was a win for your company in the past year?

Being able to continue working with Kosmos, and some other big architect-designed hemp-lime homes. I haven't done a lot of hemp block projects until this year. I am im-

> *" The biggest obstacle is changing the construction industry's outlook. "*

ENGINEERS

CA

Featured
VERDANT STRUCTURAL ENGINEERS
Contact: Anthony Dente
(510) 528-5394
Verdantstructural.com
1101 8th Street #180 Berkeley, CA 94710
admin@verdantstructural.com

BACKMAN BUILDING SERVICES - *Eureka*
Contact: Chrissy Backman, PE
Backmanbuilding.com

PIECE BY PAZ, INC. - *Los Angeles*
Contact: Wilfredo Paz Bermudez, PE
Piecebypaz.us

CO

Featured
CROWN JADE DESIGN & ENGINEERING - *Greeley*
Contact: Mark Benjamin
(970) 472-2394
Crownjade.com
PO Box 336702 Greeley, CO, 80633
Mark@crownjade.com

IM SMITH ENGINEERING - *Boulder*
Contact: Ian Smith, P.E.
Imsmith.com

LIVING CRAFT DESIGN BUILD - *Arvada*
Contact: Frank Wetenkamp
Livingcraft.design

DF SWOBODA ARCHITECTURE - *Boulder*
Contact: David Swoboda
Dfswoboda.com

Pennsylvania hempcrete home addition with custom tinted lime plaster. Photo courtesy Lancaster Lime Works

DE

Featured
HEMPBLOCK USA
Contact: Glen Donoghoe
(855) 760-0756
Hempblockusa.com
16192 Coastal Highway, Lewes, DE 19958
Admin@hempblockusa.com

MA

CAMBRIDGE SEVEN - *Cambridge*
Contact: Jacob Bloom
Cambridgeseven.com

HOMEWORKS DESIGN BUILD - *Easthampton*
Contact: Lauren Faulkner Duncan
Homeworksdesignbuild.com

NEXT PHASE STUDIOS - *Brookline*
Contact: Lisa Sun
Nps-architects.com

NY

TURNER CONSTRUCTION - *NYC*
Contact: Joel Ahearne-Ray
Turnerconstruction.com

TY-LIN - *Brooklyn*
Contact: Justin Den Herder, PE
Tylin.com

TX

STEINMAN LUEVANO STRUCTURES, L.L.P. - *Austin*
Contact: Richard Luevano
Slstructures.com

VA

DRAWING CONCLUSIONS, LLC - *Alexandria*
Contact: Valerie Amor, LEED AP, CPHD, CC-P
Valeriejamor@gmail.com

AMERICHANVRE
CAST-HEMP
HEMP BUILDING TRAINING AND INSTALLATION
HEMPCRETE WORKSHOPS WITH CAMERON MCINTOSH
SIGN UP NOW
GET EVERYTHING
YOU NEED TO GET STARTED!
TRAINING SESSIONS
✓ Assembly and operation of the Ereasy System
✓ Work-site safety and organization
✓ Spray application technique
✓ Become a certified installer
INSTALLATION
✓ Specializes in New Builds and Retrofits
✓ Professional and fast service
✓ Licensed and fully insured
EREASY + MUDHOG
EREASY® Spray Applied Hempcrete System
• EREASY® Package
EZG® Manufacturing Batch Plants
• EZG® Mud Hog MH20
• EZG® Mud Hog MH12
• EZG12
BUILDING MATERIALS
Hemp Hurd
• Certified Building Grade Hurd
• 20kg & 10kg bags
EREASY 120 Binder
• Only binder product that can be used with the Ereasy Spray Applied Hempcrete System
833-443-6727 | cameron@americhanvre.com | americhanvre.com

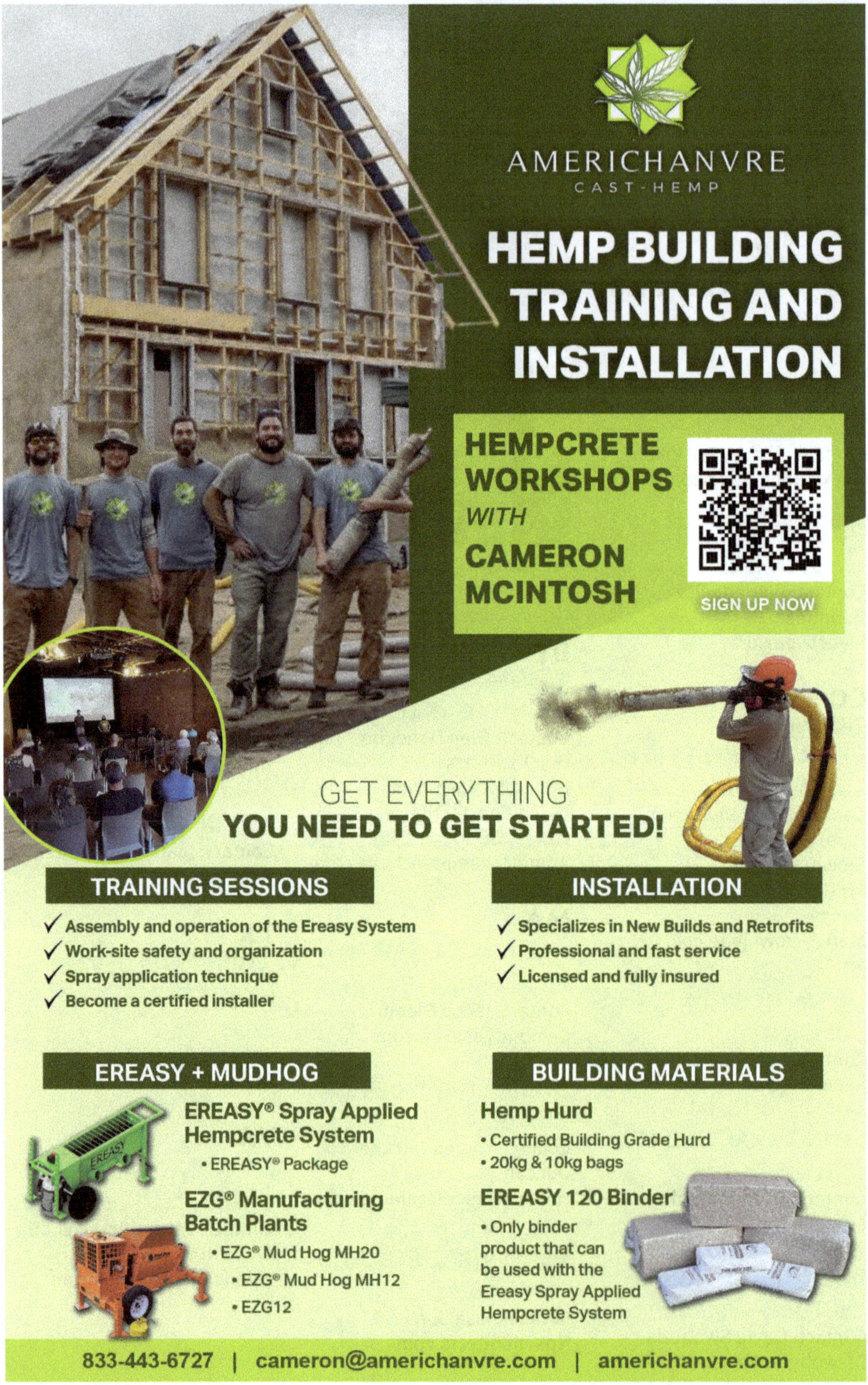

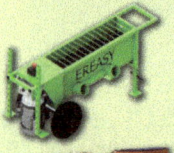

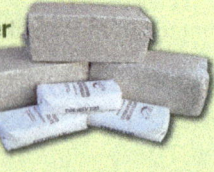

HEMPCRETE INSULATION SUBCONTRACTORS/ HEMPCRETE INSTALLERS

Spray casting hemplime with Ereasy Spray System. Photo courtesy Tim Callahan

AZ
OLD PUEBLO HEMP COMPANY - *Tucson*
Contact: Micaela Machado
Oldpueblohempco.com

CA
Featured
AARON GRAIL CONSTRUCTION
- *Sebastopol*
Aarongrailconstruction.com
Contact: Aaron Grail
(707) 292 4097
6400 Lone Pine Rd,
Sebastopol, CA 95472
Aaron@aarongrailconstruction.com

GREEN TRUTH LLC.
- *Petaluma*
Contact: David Dickson
Grntrth.com

DOTEK - *San Diego*
Contact: Chris Velasco
Thedotek.com

FARMTIVA
- *Laguna Beach*
Contact: Chris Boucher
Farmtiva.com

INDIGENOUS HABITAT INSTITUTE - *Trinidad*
Contact: Lisa Sundberg
Indigenoushabitatinstitute.com

OBSIDIAN GOLD
- *Fresno*
Contact: Elliot Bailey
Obsidiangold24@gmail.com

SOLSTICE ECO BUILDING SUPPLY
- *Joshua Tree*
Contact: Nicholas Holmes
Solsticeeco.com

DYLAN TRIMARCHI
- *Bishop*
Dylantrimarchi@gmail.com

CO
Featured
HEALTHY HEMP HOMES
- *Denver Metro*
Healthyhemphomes.org
Contact: Eric Milburn
855 Gray Street, Lakewood, CO 80214
Eric@healthyhemphomes.org
(970) 821-5461

Featured
HEMPIRE HOLDINGS CO
Hempire.tech
Contact: Sergiy Kovalenkov
+38 0676585350

Featured
EVOLVE CONSTRUCTION
- *Steamboat Springs*
Evolvehomebuild.com
Contact: Jeremy Stephen
(970) 846-3178
PO Box 772536, Steamboat Springs, CO 80477
Jeremy@Evolvehomebuild.com

HEMPCRETE INSULATION SUBCONTRACTORS/HEMPCRETE INSTALLERS

Featured
HEMP BUILDING COMPANY - Lafayette
Hempbuildingco.com
Contact: Phelan Dalton
(720) 231-6865
Info@hempbuildingco.com

HIGH DESERT HEMP HOMES - Howard
Contact: Taylus Schley
Highdeserthemphomes.com

LIVING CRAFT DESIGN BUILD - Arvada
Contact: Frank Wetenkamp
Livingcraft.design

PLASTER ARTISAN - Paonia
Contact: Kael Frank
Plasterartisan.com

FL
ABT CONSTRUCTION - Jacksonville
Contact: Andrea Troutman
Abtconstruction@aol.com

MR. HEMP HOUSE - Orlando
Contact: Chris Penn
Mrhemphouse.com

HI
HEMP CRE8 - Mt. View
Contact: Richard Lee
Hempmountainindustries@gmail.com

PERMANENTLY AFFORDABLE LIVING KAUA'I - Anahola
Contact: Glen Head
Pal-kauai.org

LA
GRO ENTERPRISES - New Orleans
Contact: Joel Holton
Groenterprises.biz

EARTHWORKS CONSTRUCTION - Baton Rouge
Contact: Nick Papalaskaris
Earthworks.homes

STRONG CONSTRUCTION - Lafayette
Contact: Joe Strong
Strong-construction.com

MA
Featured
HILLSIDE CENTER FOR SUSTAINABLE LIVING
Hillsidecenterforsustainable-living.com
2 Federal St., Newburyport, MA 01950
Contact: David Hall
office@hallandmoskow.com
(978) 465-7047

HEMPSTONE - Hatfield
Contact: Tom Rossmassler
Hempstone.net

VILLAGE CARPENTRY AND LANDSCAPING - Goshen
Contact: Shelby Howland
Villagecarpentryma.com

ME
LION CARPENTRY - Portland
Contact: Ethan Lavendier
Mainelioncarpentry@gmail.com

MD
HEMPIRE BUILDS - Annapolis
Contact: Benjamin Fisher
Hempirebuilds.com

Mixing hemp lime on a Colorado build. Photo courtesy of the Hemp Building Company

HEMPCRETE INSULATION SUBCONTRACTORS/HEMPCRETE INSTALLERS

MI

FIBERFORT
- *Madison Heights*
Contact: Kim Croes
Fiberfort.com

HEMP 4 HUMANITY
- *Detroit*
Contact: Cody Ley
H4h.earth

SUPER NATURAL STRUCTURES
- *Marquette*
Contact: Donald Samulski
Supernaturalstructures.com

WASHTENAW WOODWRIGHTS
- *Washtenaw*
Contact: Bruce Curtis
Woodwrights.com

MN

LOWER SIOUX HEMP
- *Morton*
Contact: Danny Desjarlais
Lowersioux.com

MT

BIG SKY HEMP
- *Choteau*
Contact: Doug Weist
Bigskyhemp.us

ND

Featured
HOMELAND HEMPCRETE
Homelandhempco.com
Contact: Matthew Marino
(701) 426-3796
551 Airport Rd, Bismarck, ND 58504
Matt@homelandhempcrete.com

NH

Featured
VICTURA HEMP
- *Somersworth*
Victurahemp.com
Contact: Jared Sores, Tristin Wells
(570) 447-7543
11 Lee Street, Somersworth, NH 03878
Jaredsones@victurahemp.com

NE

GENERAL HEMP CONSTRUCTION
- *Denton*
Contact: Tina Jones
Generalhempconstruction@outlook.com

NM

REFUGE INDUSTRIAL HEMP BUILDING
- *Albuquerque*
Contact: Robin Elkin
Refugehempnm@gmail.com

NY

BUILD GREEN NOW
- *Kingston*
Contact: Henry Gage
Buildgreennow.net

RONDOUT NATURAL BUILDERS - *Kingston*
Contact: Jeff Gagnon
Rondoutnaturalbuilders@gmail.com

HEMPCRETE INSULATION SUBCONTRACTORS/HEMPCRETE INSTALLERS

WOODSTOCK HEMPCRETE - *Woodstock*
Contact: Paul Petrov
Woodstockhempcrete.com

OR

FAMILY 1ST BUILDING & REMODELING - *La Pine*
Contact: Diana Forsberg
family1stbr.com

HEMPTOWN ON MAIN
- *Jacksonville*
Contact: Greg Flavell
Hemptownonmain.org

MARCUS LEIGHTY REMODEL, LLC
- *Roseburg*
Marcusleighty@gmail.com

PA
Featured
AMERICHANVRE CAST HEMP
Americhanvre.com
Contact: Cameron McIntosh
(833) 443-6727
1529 Brookside Road, Allentown, PA 18102
cameron@americhanvre.com

PERENNIAL BUILDING, LLC
- *Sisters*
Contact: Karen Rugg
Perennialbuilding.com

TN
HAVEN EARTH, PMA
- *Old Fort*
Contact: Paul River Richardson
Havenearth.biz

TX
Featured
HEMP BUILD NETWORK
New Braunfels, TX
Contact: Ray Kaderli
(540) 664-6499

BRAD KING
- *Dripping Springs*
Contact: Brad King
Bradkingbuild@gmail.co

DEL TORO NATURAL BUILDERS - *Mason*
Contact: Darren Del Toro
Deltoronaturalbuilders.com

GRADEK CONTRACTING AND DESIGNS
Gradekcontracting.com
Contact: Carl Gradek

VA
SEED TO STRUCTURE
- *Forest*
Contact: Scott McStacy
Scottmcstacy@gmail.com

VT
TREVOR GREEN
- *Huntington*
Tgreen2584@gmail.com

WA
Featured
NEXT GENESIS DESIGN
- *White Salmon*
Contact: John Hutton
(312) 339-8248
Nextgenesisdesign.com
8 Debo Road, White Salmon, WA 98672
John@Nextgenesisdesign.com

HAPPY HEALTHY HOME
- *Salmon*
Contact: Yaniv Koby
Happyhealthyhomenw.com

Using a drum mixer to mix hempcrete. Photo courtesy Tim Callahan

HEMPCRETE INSULATION SUBCONTRACTORS/HEMPCRETE INSTALLERS

LIMELIFE CONSTRUCTION
- *Chehalis*
Contact: Andrew Hancock
Drew.hancock@sbcglobal.net

NATURAL ECO BUILDERS - *Seattle*
Contact: Terrance Aaron Lee-Hammond
Naturalecobuilders@gmail.com

NORTHWEST HEMP BUILDERS
Contact: Matt Eckland
Nwhempbuilders@g mail.com

STEENPAD
- *Bainbridge Island*
Contact: Klaas Hesselink
Steenpad.com

WI

Featured
SATIVA BUILDING SYSTEMS
Sativabuildingsystems.com
Contact: Zachery Popp
(715) 470-0677
N6416 Banner Road
Wittenberg, WI 54499
info@sativabuildingsystems.com

WV

SEVEN RIVERS DESIGN BUILD
- *Hillsboro*
Contact: Andrew Must
Sevenriversdesignbuild.com

HEADWATERS HEMP
- *Hillsboro*
Contact: Clay Condon
Headwatersdb.com

Cameron McIntosh of Americhanvre (L) poses at a hempcrete home in Drake, CO. Photo courtesy of Jean Lotus

LEADER PROFILE

JARED SONES & TRISTIN WELLS
Hempcrete Buildings Last for Generations

As co-owners of a small business, our responsibilities often intersect. However, Tristin concentrates on design and development, while Jared manages operations.

Hemp intrigues us because it aligns with our focus on thinking beyond the moment a building goes up, considering the third and fourth lives of the structure's inhabitants. It's an incredible material to work with, responding terrifically to the forms and demands we ask of it.

What was a win for your company in the past year?

A key win was developing and using our modular panel in a small Weymouth, MA studio. Attending the International Hemp Building Symposium was also a privilege, where we met industry leaders and were proudly introduced as the New England hemp builders.

Jared: I learned our friends in Germany were growing winter hemp, planted in July and harvested the following spring. I thought this was a brilliant way to get farmers on board without disrupting their summer crops. **Tristin:** I initially dismissed "hippie-hemp energy," but I now see it as a serious, research-driven movement by PhDs, adopted by top architects and builders. My view on hemp's innovation and potential has been completely recalibrated.

What bottlenecks have you observed in the industrial hemp industry and how would you solve them?

Tristin Wells (L) & Jared Sones (R) are co-founders of New Hampshire-based Victura Hemp.

Jared: Building a robust Northeast supply chain is challenging due to a shortage of growers and processors. Farmers are hesitant without established processing, and specialized harvesting equipment is a barrier. Securing dedicated long-term investors is a difficult but necessary solution. **Tristin:** While supply chain issues exist, the main bottleneck is public perception. Hemp still faces misconceptions—I'm still asked if a burning house will get people high. To overcome this distrust and connotation, my plan is to keep building. The more people who experience these hemp structures—feeling the quiet, comfort, and air quality—we can dispel these misunderstandings firsthand.

LEADER PROFILE
CAMERON MCINTOSH
Hemp is a Rapidly, Annually and Agriculturally Renewable Feedstock

What most interests me about hemp building is that we are using a rapidly, annually and agriculturally renewable feedstock to insulate homes. This is an opportunity to create modern, healthy and high-performing homes for people all across the US.

What was a win for your company in the past year?

Last year, we insulated five residential homes in Minnesota, Virginia, North Carolina and Colorado with the home in Rochester, Minnesota being our largest single family residential home to date and the second largest hempcrete home in the country. We expanded our network of Ereasy system owner operators, which now includes Cornell Universities Agricultural program thanks to one of our original Ereasy system trainees, Henry Gage, Jr., who brought a plan to Dr. Larry Smart at Cornell to purchase and make available for rent a full set of Ereasy equipment to our trained Ereasy technicians in the southern tier of New York!

Cameron McIntosh (M) pictured with Damien Baumer (L) and Danny Desjarlais (R) is founder and co-owner of Allentown, PA-based Americhanvre Cast Hemp with his wife Melissa McIntosh.

Our owner-operators are beginning to hit their stride as well, like Aaron Grail, who completed a remarkable ADU with Dylan Trimarchi in Bishop, CA.

We also successfully completed our direct to phase II U.S. Army SBIR work which culminated in our ASTM E119 fire resistance data being included in IRC Appendix BL with the help of Hempbuild Magazine and a series of awesome donors.

Finally, we co-hosted the the 13th annual International Hemp Building Symposium with our owner operators, the Lower Sioux Indian Community, in Morton, MN where we demonstrated the speed and consistency of the Ereasy system for 250 attendees from around the world by spraying a hempcrete tipi designed by Homeland Hempcrete. Last year was one of our most productive, successful and intense years of operation - the work we were able to complete and the continued growth of our company and network of qualified owner operators brings a sense of accomplishment and hope for the future!

LEADER PROFILE

NAVID HATFIELD
Humans and Hemp have Co-Evolved

Our company's focus is on building positive relationships with our homes and landscapes through natural building (hempcrete, lime and clay plasters), regenerative design and practices, and plant/tree/soil health with mineralization and applied microbiology.

I have been a cannabis activist since my first experiences with it as a teen. After reading Jack Herer's *The Emperor Wears no Clothes* at age 14, I realized that we have co-evolved with this plant for tens of thousands of years and that within her deep genetic treasure she holds the gifts of food, clothing, housing, and medicine.

Fast-forward to the 2018 farm bill and I was growing MDAR licensed minor cannabinoids at a financial loss and connecting to other hempcrete enthusiasts. Soon after, I was building with hempcrete in Cape Cod, Hudson NY and Putney VT, and later Morton MN. I had the honor of collaborating with HempStone, Americhanvre, and the Lower Sioux hemp crew among others.

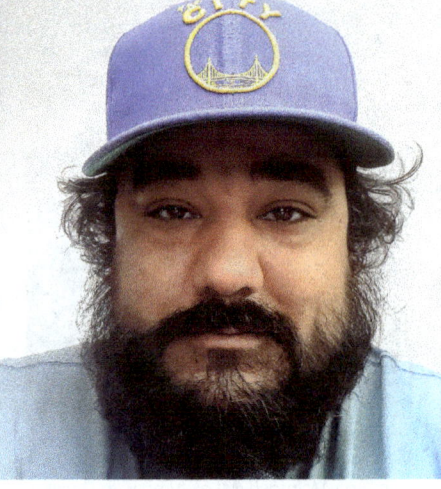

Navid Hatfield owns and operates Pioneer Valley Organics, a permaculture and organic landcare business in Amherst MA.

The hemp highlight of the year is a tie between two hemp projects. The first is a HempStone project in NYC. Installing hemp blocks in an 1800's brownstone. It was a revelation that we could infiltrate the depths of the city with our agricultural product and create an impact within urban environments in thousands of homes.

The second has to be the 13th International Hemp Symposium at the Lower Sioux community in MN. I met an incredible group of humans from around the world, all focused in their own way on making the world better through hemp and bio building.

The greatest barrier to hempcrete in the U.S. is undoubtedly psychological. It is the psychological trauma of prohibition that blinds the political will to subsidize hemp like any other high-value ag product.

PLASTERERS

Colorado plaster workshop with Frank Wetenkamp, Living Craft Design Build. Photo by Jean Lotus

CA
SOLSTICE ECO BUILDING SUPPLY
- *Joshua Tree*
Contact: Nicholas Holmes
Solsticeeco.com

CO
INFINITE CROWMA
- *Alamosa*
Contact: Cari Conari
Infinitecrowma@gmail.com

LIVING CRAFT DESIGN BUILD - *Arvada*
Contact: Frank Wetenkamp
Livingcraft.design

PLASTER ARTISAN
- *Paonia*
Contact: Kael Frank
Plasterartisan.com

Q CREATIONS
- *Woodland Park*
Contact: Quinton Montgomery
Q-creations.com

CT
JOHN CANNING & CO
- *Cheshire*
Contact: David Riccio
Johncanningco.com

IA
TIM WHITE, NATURAL BUILDER - *Waukon*
Contact: Tim White
Texashealthyhomes.com

MA
Featured
HILLSIDE CENTER FOR SUSTAINABLE LIVING
Hillsidecenterforsustainable-living.com
Contact: David Hall
(978) 465-7047
2 Federal St., Newburyport, MA 01950
Office@hallandmoskow.com

D.P. AUTIO CO. - *Littleton*
Contact: DP
Dpautioornamentalplaster.com

MN
Featured
EARTHHAUS PLASTER
- *Duluth*
Contact: Ryan Chivers
Admin@earthausplaster.com
(800) 917-2414
Earthausplaster.com

MT
PLEASANT CREEK PLASTER - *Connor*
Contact: Bill Bradbury
Enviroconutah@gmail.com

OR
GOLD HILL CLAY PLASTER - *Gold Hill*
Contact: James Henderson
Goldhillclayplaster.com

PLASTERERS LOCAL 82
- *Portland*
Contact: Kevin Hess-Natemeier
Plastererslocal82.com

PLASTERERS • FINANCIAL SERIVCES • HEMP BUILDING/NEWS/PUBLIC RELATIONS • TRANSPORTATION

PA
THE ART OF PLASTER
- *Black Eddy*
Contact: Gabriel Franklin
Theartofplaster.com

LIMEWORKS US - *Telford*
Contact: Daniel Christiansen
Limeworks.us

SC
REAL FINISHES
- *Charleston*
Contact: Patrick Webb
Realfinishes.com

TX
BIOLIME, LLC
- *Woodway*
Contact: Brian Coia
Biolime.com

BRAD KING
- *Dripping Springs*
Contact: Brad King
Bradkingbuild@gmail.com

DEL TORO NATURAL BUILDERS - *Mason*
Contact: Darren Del Toro
Deltoronaturalbuilders.com

TEXAS COB - *Kingsbury*
Contact: Simon Gonzalez
Texascob.com

MT
PLEASANT CREEK PLASTER - *Richmond*
Contact: Bill Bradbury
Enviroconutah@gmail.com

WA
STEENPAD
- *Bainbridge Island*
Contact: Klaas Hesselink
Steenpad.com

FINANCIAL SERVICES

NC
FIRST CITIZENS BANK
- *Raleigh*
firstcitizens.com

VT
QUANTIFIED VENTURES
- *Montpelier*
Contact: Mike Crowley
Quantifiedventures.com

NY
REPLANT HEMP ADVISORS - *NYC*
Contact: Wilson Kello
Replanthemp.com

TRANSPORTATION

FL
US1 LOGISTICS
- *Ponte Vedra Beach*
Contact: Chris Kinsel
Us1network.com

HEMP BUILDING NEWS/PUBLIC RELATIONS

CO
HEMPBUILD MAGAZINE
- *Fort Collins*
Contact: Jean Lotus
Hempbuildmag.com

HEMPTODAY
- *Poland*
Contact: Kehrt Reyher
Hemptoday.net

MI
HOMESTEADING COPYWRITER - *Otsego*
Contact: Jackie Smith
Homesteadingcopywriter.com

Hempcrete Workshop at Hemp Building Company. Photo by Jean Lotus

LEADER PROFILE

DANNY DESLARLAIS
Education for Underserved Communities and Seed to Sovereignty

Green Buffalo Institute is a majority indigenous women-run nonprofit with the goal of bringing natural building education to the underserved communities. Just getting the 501(c)3 status and our documentation from the IRS December 30th was a huge success especially with the government shutdown right after we submitted the paperwork. We are focused on addressing the lack of educational opportunities for the underserved communities with a strong focus on our indigenous communities.

For the Lower Sioux Industrial Hemp Construction Program, I oversee the entire process from seed to sovereignty.

A win for us in the past year was hosting the 13th International Hemp Building Symposium in October and completing our first project off of the reservation in Rochester with Americhanvre.

Our bottleneck at the Lower Sioux is definitely processing – which I feel is pretty similar to the rest of the US industrial hemp industry. We are looking to upgrade and expand our processing production but don't want to put any more funding towards a subpar equipment line. We have taken a step back from processing in hopes someone else in the US will find the solution. We have focused more on offsite construction and will be offering our panel system to other communities in the spring of 2026.

Danny Desjarlais is founder and board member for the Green Buffalo Institute and director of the Lower Sioux Industrial Hemp Construction Program.

HEMP BUILDING DIRECTORY 2026

LEADER PROFILE

JOHAN TIJSSEN
Hempcrete Completely Changed My 30-year Building Career!

Johan "T" Tijssen - founder of HempBLOCK International.

As a building contractor for 30 years, the best thing that could have happened to me was discoveing HEMPCRETE. After 20 years building, training builders and doing countless hours of R&D, I developed the easy-to-use LB 300 HempBLOCK load-bearing walling system. It is faster and more cost-competitive than conventional systems, while requiring fewer specialized skills. Impotantly, it delivers truly energy-efficient buildings with superior performance in occupant safety, health, and comfort.

What was a win for your company in the past year?

In the last year, we doubled our turnover and achieved the world's only certified 3-hour HempBLOCK fire rating for our proprietary LB 300 walling system.

What bottlenecks have you observed in the industrial hemp industry and how would you solve them?

One of the biggest challenges is the perception that HempBLOCK construction is complex, expensive, and limited in its use.

Our focus is to prove its versatility by demonstrating how LB 300 HempBLOCKs are used in large-scale projects and deliver practical, and commercially viable walling systems.

> " HempBLOCK provides the opportunity to live in safe, healthy and sustainable buildings "

CHAPTER 4

HEMP PRODUCT MANUFACTURERS

MN Adopts Hempcrete in Residential Building Codes

By Jean Lotus and Martin Hammer

Last year, Minnesota was the first US state on the path to adopting hemp-lime ("hempcrete") in state building codes.

The state's Technical Advisory Group (TAG) to the Construction Codes Advisory Council in St. Paul approved adoption of Appendix BL of the 2024 International Residential Codes (IRC), voting 8-1 in favor.

"When we walked out of the hearing we were hugging and high-fiving and screaming," Danny Desjarlais, head of the hempcrete team at the Lower Sioux Community in southwestern Morton, MN told Hemp-Build Mag.

Desjarlais credited an international "Dream Team" of more than 20 local and North American architects, engineers and building-science pros committed to using non-toxic natural bio-based materials. "They did all the hard work," Desjarlais said. The North Star State has been a center of

Minneapolis strawbale home designer, Janneke Schaap (L) high-fives Danny Desjarlais of the Lower Sioux Hempcrete Group (R) after the first approval of natural building appendices in the Minnesota state residential building codes. Photo courtesy of Simona Fischer, AIA.

US hempcrete construction activity and activism mostly thanks to the determination of the Lower Sioux, of one of the nation's tiniest tribal communities. Tribe members, with a home-grown hempcrete team, have already built four hempcrete homes on their reservation, largely from hemp grown and processed on site. The Lower Sioux received a nearly $5 million grant in 2024 from the US Environmental Protection Agency to renovate 30 homes with hempcrete on the reservation. Why so much excitement over an arcane building code tweak? Adopting natural building methods into the official state code means cutting red tape for builders, designers and homeowners, making things much more affordable to build a hempcrete or strawbale home. Plus, these determinations come around in cycles, and the next chance to adopt new codes would be in 2031.

Still need final approval
The code changes still need to be finally approved by the state building officials at the overarching agency, the Minnesota Department of Labor and Industry. But advocates believe that will soon happen. The hard work is done. Online, architect Koosman called the decision a "major victory" and added, "Minnesota homeowners, builders and building officials can now simplify the permitting process for safe, durable and healthy homes."

Minnesota's "dream team" members achieved a win for strawbale and hempcrete adoption. L-R Janneke Schaap, Simona Fischer, AIA, Anna Koosmann, AIA Rep. Katie Jones, Danny Desjarlais. Photo courtesy of Katie Jones

BUILD SMARTER

Why Choose HempBLOCKs?
- Online estimator tools
- US HempBLOCK installer training
- No special equipment needed
- Fast, smart & cost effective design & engineering service

Benefits for You and Your Clients:
- **Eco-Friendly:** Low waste, natural, carbon-negative
- **Durable:** Insulates, breathes, resists mould
- **Safe & Healthy:** Fire & termite-resistant, VOC-free
- **Faster Builds:** 1- blocks, 2 - post & beams, 3 - stucco, quick and simple

Ready To Build Fast, Clean & GREEN?
www.hempblockusa.com | Scan the QR for more info

Hempcrete panel home built by Morton, MN Lower Sioux with panels by Homeland Hempcrete. Photo courtesy of Matt Marino.

HEMP BLOCK SYSTEMS

AZ

OLD PUEBLO HEMP CO
- Tucson
Contact: Micaela Machado
Oldpueblohempco.com

QUADRA-USA - *Phoenix*
Contact: Pascal Allain
Quadra-concrete.com

CA

DTE MATERIALS
- Fresno
Contact: Jose Urizar
Dtematerials.com

CO

Featured
HEMP BUILDING COMPANY - *Lafayette*
Hempbuildingco.com
Contact: Phelan Dalton
(720) 231-6865
Info@hempbuildingco.com

Featured
NATURALIA CONSTRUCTION - *Alamosa*
Naturaliaconstruction.com
Contact: Gamal Jadue Zalaquette
610 State Ave, Alamosa, CO 81401
Hello@naturaliaconstruction.com

HEMP AND BLOCK, LLC
- Montrose
Contact: Derek Wolf
Hempandblock.com

DE

Featured
HEMPBLOCK USA
Hempblockusa.com
Contact: Glen Donoghoe
(855) 760-0756
16192 Coastal Highway, Lewes, DE 19958
Admin@hempblockusa.com

FL

MR. HEMP HOUSE
- Orlando
Contact: Chris Penn
Mrhemphouse.com

IA

TIM WHITE, NATURAL BUILDER - *Waukon*
Contact: Tim White
Texashealthyhomes.com

ID

Featured
HEMPITECTURE, INC.
Hempitecture.com
Contact: Mattie Mead
(208) 218-8698
421 E 500 S #100, Jerome, ID 83338
Mattie@hempitecture.com

Tamping hempcrete in a wall form. Photo courtesy of Tim Callahan.

HEMP BLOCK SYSTEMS

MN
LOWER SIOUX HEMP
- Morton
Contact: Danny Desjarlais
Lowersioux.com

PA
COEXIST BUILD, LLC
- Blandon
Contact: Ana Konopitskaya
Coexist.build

TX
Featured
CANNAVISION, INC
- Fort Worth
Cannavisioninc.com
Contact: David Russell
(833) 284-4367
4501 CR 312 B, Cleburne, TX 76031
lhp@cannavisioninc.com

WA
EARTH MERCHANT
- Vancouver
Contact: Gina Engel
Earthmerchant.com

WI
Featured
SATIVA BUILDING SYSTEMS
Sativabuildingsystems.com
Contact: Zachery Popp
(715) 470-0677
N6416 Banner Road
Wittenberg, WI 54499

Brick mason Larry Hill of Bricklayers Local.

LEADER PROFILE

ZACH POPP
Hemp Material Can Make Buildings Better

Sativa Building Systems has been manufacturing hempcrete Z panels since 2022 along with tiny homes. In the last 2 years we have expanded into also performing research and development and offering construction services.

I love the performance potential of hemp and all bio-based materials. Building safer, healthier, and more energy efficient buildings has always been our core mission, and hemp building materials are a key component in making buildings better.

What was a win for your company in the past year?

We completed a Z Panel installation on a large residential project and it went great. The opportunity to test our products on a more complex project helped validate the functionality and versatility of our precast hempcrete panels. We also completed several ASTM tests on a new hemp-mycelium material, and several yielded very promising results, including a class A fire rating.

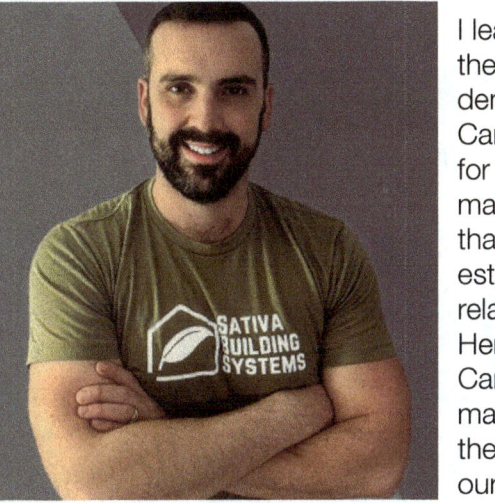

Zach Popp is founder and president of Sativa Building Systems in Wittenberg, WI.

What is something about hemp/natural building/construction/processing you didn't know a year ago?

I learned that there is a healthy demand in the Canadian market for hemp building materials. We are thankful to have established a relationship with Hemp Homes Canada for the manufacturing and the distribution of our Z Panels.

What bottlenecks have you observed in the natural building/hemp industry and how would you solve them?

Awareness is the ongoing challenge. Potential customers often have to sort through products that are in an idea-stage from those that are market-ready. This can cloud the market, and make it more challenging for businesses that are ready to serve customers to actually reach them.

BUILDING HEALTHY HOMES
SUSTAINABLE LIVING STARTS TODAY

Hempcrete Z Panel walls are.....

- Fire Resistant ✓
- Mold Resistant ✓
- Pest Resistant ✓
- Rot Resistant ✓
- Fully Code Approved ✓

0 TOXINS
3X LONGER LIFESPAN
50% ENGERY SAVINGS

SATIVA BUILDING SYSTEMS

sativabuildingsystems.com

HEMP PANEL SYSTEMS

CA

BRIGHTWORKS SUSTAINABILITY NETWORK - *Oakland*
Contact: Heath Blount
Brightworks.net

CARBONL3SS MODULAR - *Los Angeles*
Contact: Wilfredo Paz Bermudez, PE
Piecebypaz.us

FACTORY_OS - *Vallejo*
Contact: Rick Holliday
Factoryos.com

INDIGENOUS HABITAT INSTITUTE - *Trinidad*
Contact: Lisa Sundberg
Indigenoushabitatinstitute.com

KREYSLER & ASSOCIATES - *American Canyon*
Contact: William Kreysler
Kreysler.com

CO
Featured
EVOLVE CONSTRUCTION - *Steamboat Springs*
Evolvehomebuild.com
Contact: Jeremy Stephen
(970) 846-3178
PO Box 772536, Steamboat Springs, CO 80477
Jeremy@Evolvehomebuild.com

CITIZENS FOR CLEAN ENERGY - *Durango*
Contact: Steve Heising
Citizensforcleanenergy.org

DC
Featured
BISON BIOCOMPOSITES
Bisonbiocomposites.com
Contact: Chad Frey
402-650-5032
318 Massachusetts Ave NE, Washington, DC 20002
Info@bisonbiocomposites.com

IL
US HERITAGE GROUP
Contact: Tai Olson
Usheritage.com

MA
Featured
HILLSIDE CENTER FOR SUSTAINABLE LIVING
Hillsidecenterforsustainable-living.com
Contact: David Hall
(978) 465-7047
2 Federal St., Newburyport, MA 01950
Office@hallandmoskow.com

MO
TIGER FIBER HEMP - *St. Louis*
Contact: James Forbes
Tigerfiberhemp.com

MN
LOWER SIOUX HEMP - *Morton*
Contact: Danny Desjarlais
Lowersioux.com

OR
HEMPTOWN ON MAIN - *Jacksonville*
Contact: Greg Flavell
Hemptownonmain.org

ND
Featured
HOMELAND HEMPCRETE
Homelandhempco.com
Contact: Matthew Marino
(701) 426-3796
551 Airport Rd, Bismarck, ND 58504
Matt@Homelandhempcrete.com

WI
Featured
SATIVA BUILDING SYSTEMS
Sativabuildingsystems.com
Contact: Zachery Popp
(715) 470-0677
N6416 Banner Road ·Wittenberg, WI 54499
Zach@sativapanel.com

HEMP BUILDING DIRECTORY 2026

LEADER PROFILE

GREGORY WILSON
Bioconstruction is about Working with Nature Rather than Against it

My role is to guide the company's vision, oversee operations, and drive innovation in sustainable building materials.

What excites me most is the potential to redefine what sustainable construction can look like. Hemp is incredibly versatile, fast-growing, and regenerative—it can absorb carbon, restore soils, and produce durable building materials. Bioconstruction, broadly, is about working with nature rather than against it, and that philosophy is at the heart of HempWood. Knowing that every project using hemp can help reduce the environmental footprint of construction keeps me inspired.

Gregory Wilson is founder and CEO of Murray, KY-based HempWood.

What was a win for your company in the past year?

One of our biggest wins was our production growth, making HempWood more accessible to builders, architects, and homeowners. This year in fact, HempWood was recognized by *Inc.* as the fastest-growing manufacturer in Kentucky, all while we were able to keep the same crew.

It's people who make the difference. Each year, I discover more about the world of sustainability and the companies driving it. It's inspiring to see how we're all in this together, and how the industry is developing and adapting to the ever-changing economic climate.

What bottlenecks have you observed in the industrial hemp industry and how would you solve them?

One major bottleneck is the knowledge of hemp within the green building industry. Education is key; helping builders and architects understand hemp's benefits and applications accelerates the adoption of HempWood and other hemp-based materials into modern construction.

> " *It's inspiring to see how we're all in this together...* "

Truly Sustainable, High Performance, Hemp Fiber Insulation.

hempitecture®

BATT | BOARD | BLOWABLE | HEMPCRETE

www.hempitecture.com
GROWN AND MANUFACTURED IN THE USA

HEMPWOOD
ORGANIC FLOORING

- Durable in Any Space
- Soy-Based Formula
- Healthy & Non-Toxic
- Made in the USA
- Carbon Negative
- Zero-VOC

HEALTHY FLOORING, FURNITURE, AND CABINETRY

HempWood.com

LEADER PROFILE

MATT MARINO
The Best Way to Optimize is to Standardize

Our company specializes in offsite construction and fabricating SHIPs (Structural Hemp-Insulated Panels). Additionally, we offer consulting on hemp projects, and facilitate education/workshops focused on hemp building.

What originally got us excited about hemp is the opportunity to use a single plant to create many solutions. In construction, it is interesting to see how versatile the material is in different regions/climates. We are using the same material in all of our projects across the country, with minor differences in detailing, hempcrete performs well across the board.

Matt Marino is co-founder and CEO of Bismarck, ND-based Homeland Hempcrete.

What was a win for your company in the past year?

We set a company record on install where we went from foundation to fully "dried in" in 4 days on a 2-story build.

What is something about hemp/natural building/construction/processing you didn't know a year ago?

Plaster finish is rarely an easy choice. Many of our projects reduce or forgo the use of plaster due to high costs and limited labor force. Plaster is still the best option for hempcrete finish and so we have been testing some ways to make it easier and more affordable to incorporate into the build.

What bottlenecks have you observed in the hemp building industry and how would you solve them?

For us, the best way to optimize is to standardize. Our goal is to create a network of specialists that have worked with our product to help streamline the process which will save time and lower the costs for clients.

HEMP CEMENT/HARDWOOD/FLOORING/OSB/FIBERBOARD/PLYWOOD/BATT INSULATION

HEMP CEMENT

GEOPOLYMER SOLUTIONS - *Conroe, TX*
Contact: Rod Zubrod
Geopolymertech.com

HEMPCEMENT CO.
- *Newport Beach, CA*
Contact: Serena Overhoff
Hempcement.co

HEMPCOAT, TAPELESS HEMP DRYWALL COMPOUND - *MN*
Contact: Adam White
Hempcoat.net

HEMP HARDWOOD/FLOORING

Featured
HEMPWOOD®
- *Murray KY*
Contact: Greg Wilson
(888) 338-1235
Sales@hempwood.com
Hempwood.com
301 Rockwood Rd, Murray, KY 42071

HEMP OSB/FIBERBOARD/PLYWOOD

Featured
BOARDWURKS - *New Smyrna Beach, FL*
Boardwurks.com
Contact: Miles Gathright
(386) 576-3800
1500 Palmetto St., New Smyrna Beach, FL 32168
Miles@boardwwurks.com

Featured
HEMPWOOD®
- *Murray KY*
Hempwood.com
Contact: Greg Wilson
(888) 338-1235
301 Rockwood Rd, Murray, KY 42071
Sales@hempwood.com

FOREVERBOARD - *Shafter, CA*
Contact: Ronald Voit
Foreverboard.net

HEMP BATT INSULATION

Featured
HEMPITECTURE, INC.
Hempitecture.com
Contact: Mattie Mead
(208) 218-8698
421 E 500 S #100, Jerome, ID 83338

128 Hemp Building Directory | 2026

HEMP BUILDING DIRECTORY 2026

LEADER PROFILE

MILES GATHRIGHT
Landfill Avoidance and Decarbonization Drive Me

I am the technical lead at Boardwurks when it comes to manufacturing sheet goods from plant-based and recycled materials. I also consult with manufacturing companies in respect to landfill avoidance and decarbonization.

The ability of hemp to sequester carbon and its carbon-negative status is most interesting to me.

What was a win for your company in the past year?

Boardwurks initiated building material certification for plant based structural panels.

What is something about hemp building/construction/processing you didn't know a year ago?

We have just learned how to make a panel that can achieve a Class-A fire rating.

Miles Gathright is owner/operator at Boardwurks Biocomposites, based in New Smyrna Beach FL

What bottlenecks have you observed in the industrial hemp industry/natural building industry and how would you solve them?

Scale is needed to reduce cost but will not happen until there are more high-volume building material applications. Boardwurks Biocomposites and partners will be establishing manufacturing facilities for structural panels in the near future.

> " We have just learned how to make a panel that can achieve a Class-A fire rating. "

2026 | Hemp Building Directory **129**

HEMP WALLPAPER/STAINS & RESINS/PLASTIC

Mattie@hempitecture.com
GREEN FOX LLC - *South Haven, MN*
Contact: Ellie Fox
Greenfoxcompanies.com

TIGER FIBER HEMP - *St. Louis, MO*
Contact: James Forbes
Tigerfiberhemp.com

HEMP WALLPAPER

PURE HEMP NY
- *Hudson NY*
Contact: Ralph Brill
Brill.group@verizon.net

HEMP STAINS AND RESINS

HEMP SHIELD
- *Eugene, OR*
Contact: Steve Nisewander
Hempshields.com

THE REAL MILK PAINT COMPANY
- *Hohenwald, TN*
Realmilkpaint.com
Contact: Dwayne Siever

SMART BIOHEMP
- *Hagerstown, MD*
Contact: Michael Baughman
Smartbiohemp.com

VERMONT NATURAL COATINGS
- *Hardwick, VT*
Contact: Andrew Meyer
Vermontnaturalcoatings.com

HEMP PLASTIC

THE HEMP PLASTIC COMPANY - *Boulder, CO*
Contact: Caroline
Hempplastic.com

IHEMPMICHIGAN
- *Ferrysburg, MI*
Contact: Dave Crabill
Ihempmichigan.com

Plastering a hempcrete home. Photo courtesy Tim Callahan.

LEADER PROFILE

CHAD FREY
Our Material Met the Real World This Year

I spend significant time educating builders, manufacturers, developers, and regulators about the benefits of hemp materials. Some of my other roles include capital strategy, fundraising, and financial management.

I grew up on a struggling farm in Nebraska, and I've seen what happens when rural communities get left behind. Hemp building materials let us do something revolutionary - turn domestic farms into climate solution infrastructure while creating an economy people can actually build their lives around.

What was a win for your company in the past year?

Chad Frey is president of DC-based Bison Biocomposites.

2025 was the year our material left the lab and met the real world. We poured pilot panels with multiple precast concrete manufacturers, collaborating with two of the largest precasters on the East Coast. Developed hemp blocks with a large-scale block plant in the Midwest. Supplied materials for 10+ new home builds. Most importantly, this was the year our material stopped being an idea and started becoming infrastructure.

What is something about hemp/natural building/construction/processing you didn't know a year ago?

Carbon removal and the MRV (monitoring, reporting, verification) infrastructure around it have become a multi-billion-dollar marketplace. Companies like Microsoft, Stripe and others are desperate for high-quality, verifiable carbon removal they can count toward their commitments. Embodied carbon in buildings is one of the few places where we can claim permanent sequestration at scale.

> *Hemp building materials let us do something revolutionary—turn domestic farms into climate solution infrastructure while creating an economy people can actually build their lives around.*

LEADER PROFILE

MATTHEW MEAD
Scaling Biobased Hemp Fiber Insulation in North America

It's been a long road at Hempitecture, one that started in my college dorm room as a student studying architecture, but it's only made possible by the small-but-mighty team we have, from the manufacturing floor to an office level.

We spend a considerable amount of our lives indoors, over 90%, and buildings and their operations are responsible for nearly 40% of our domestic carbon footprint. Whether it be displacing formaldehyde laden materials, materials that contain high amounts of plastics, or materials that off-gas VOC's - biobased materials represent a solution. You don't need to be a climatologist to understand that biobased materials that don't put things into the atmosphere, but rather, take things out– which results in a net positive. Beyond that, biomaterials can contribute to rural economic vitality.

Matthew "Mattie" Mead is CEO and co-founder of Ketchum, ID-based Hempitecture, Inc.

A win for our company was a community investment round where we were empowered to continue growing with the support of over 800 individual retail investors. I think the natural building industry runs up against a few common concerns: cost, mainstream applicability, and performance. In regards to cost, it takes time to drive cost out of processes and products, and it is possible to meet more competitive price targets. Biomaterials are not new globally, but are seen as new and early in the US. Making materials is a process that requires continuous improvement, and our products are not yet done evolving, and we look forward to continuing to share that story with our customers, partners, and stakeholders.

> "Biobased materials represent a solution—materials that don't put things into the atmosphere, but rather take things out, resulting in a net positive."

CHAPTER 5

RESEARCHERS
ACADEMIC STUDIES
TESTING AGENCIES

ACADEMIC LISTINGS & TESTING AGENCIES

A selection of publicly available academic research investigating hemp building materials with contact information for researchers.

■ Abdellatef, Yaser. University of Ottawa. yabde079@uottawa.ca - "Mechanical, Thermal, and Moisture Buffering Properties of Novel Insulating Hemp-Lime Composite Building Materials" 2020 Materials

■ Arehart, Jay. University of Colorado, Boulder. jay.arehart@colorado.edu - "On the theoretical carbon storage and carbon sequestration potential of hempcrete" 2020, Journal of Cleaner Production

■ Bartholomé, Susanne. Dept. of Engineering, Research Group "Bio-Raw Materials" Hochschule Mersberg/Hanffaser Geiseltal eG, Germany. susanne.bartholome@hs-merseburg.de

■ Ben-Alon, Lola. Columbia University GSAPP Natural Materials Lab rlb2211@columbia.edu

■ Berardi, Umberto. Ryerson University, Canada. uberardi@ryerson.ca - "Hygrothermal performance of hempcrete for Ontario (Canada) buildings" 2017, Journal of Cleaner Production

■ Calabria-Holley, Julia. University of Bath. J.C.Holley@bath.ac.uk - "Resilient hemp shiv aggregates with engineered hygroscopic properties for the building industry" 2019 Construction and Building Materials

■ Collet, Florence. Université de Rennes1, France. florence.collet@univ-rennes1.fr - "Thermal conductivity of hemp concretes: Variation with formulation, density and water content," 2014 Construction Building Materials

■ Dhakal, Ujwal. Ryerson University, Canada. ujwal.dhakal@ryerson.ca - "Hygrothermal performance of hempcrete for Ontario (Canada) buildings" 2017 Journal of Cleaner Production

■ Di Capua, Salvatore. University of Perugia, Italy. - "Evaluation of the Environmental Sustainability of Hemp as a Building Material, through Life Cycle Assessment" 2021 Environmental and Climate Technologies

■ Esau, Rebecca, et al. Rocky Mountain Institute (RMI), Boulder CO. "Embodied Carbon 101: Building Materials" 2023, RMI

■ Gibson, Michael. Kansas State University. mdgibson@ksu.edu Hemp-lime graduate seminar Dept. of Architecture, in the College of Architecture, Planning, and Design. 2023

■ Gibson, Pandwe. Massachusetts Institute of Technology, Media Lab. pandwe@ecotechvisions.com "Mainstreaming precast and block hempcrete—a carbon sequestering solution for the built environment" 2024 Academia Materials Science

■ Jami, Tarun. Central Building Research Institute, Roorkee, Uttarakhand, India. hello@greenjams.org - "Hemp Concrete – A Traditional and Novel Green Building Material" 2018 Conference: International Conference on Advances in Construction Materials and Structures

■ Jothilingam, M. SRM Institute of Science & Technology, India. lingam7907@gmail.com - "Study on strength and microstructure of hempcrete" 2019 AIP Conference Proceedings

■ Kavgic, Miroslava. University of Ottawa. mkavgic@uottawa.ca - "Temperature Control to Improve Performance of Hempcrete-Phase Change Material Wall Assemblies in a Cold Climate" 2021, Energies

■ Kinnane, Oliver. Queen's University, Belfast, Northern Ireland. o.kinnane@qub.ac.uk "Acoustic absorption of hemp-lime construction" 2016 Construction and Building Materials

■ Knapen, Elke. Hasselt University, Belgium. Elke.Knapen@uhasselt.be "Thermal performance of real-life in-situ cast lime hemp walls in Flanders" 2020 IOP Conference Series: Earth and Environmental Science

■ Latif, Eshrar. Welsh School of Architecture, Cardiff University. LatifE@cardiff.ac.uk "Experimental Analysis of Moisture-Dependent Thermal Conductivity, and Hygric Properties of Novel Hemp–shive Insulations..." 2024 Materials

NY Researchers Adapt Industrial Machinery for Plant Fibers

By Jean Lotus

An industrial hemp research team at Rensselaer Polytechnic Institute (RPI) in Troy, NY is building a state-funded manufacturing laboratory designed to bridge the gap between raw hemp fiber and industry. Part of RPI's Seed to City Initiative, the project is led by Alexandros Tsamis, director of the Center for Architecture Science and Ecology (CASE), and Daniel Walczyk, Co-Director of the RPI New York Fashion Innovation Center.

"Seed to City is about turning plants into buildings," Tsamis said. "Right now, the construction industry is one of the biggest contributors to carbon emissions, and people are asking for cleaner, healthier, low-carbon ways to build," Tsamis explained. "But the supply chain for renewable materials doesn't exist at scale yet. [This] is designed to fill that gap."

Instead of developing entirely new, niche machinery, the team is equipping the lab with standard industrial equipment typically used for petroleum-based synthetics like fiberglass and carbon fiber. The goal is to modify these established systems to accept natural fibers. Once the lab is operational, RPI plans to invite leaders from the textiles, nonwovens, and building materials sectors to witness these bio-based production lines.

"New York State is uniquely positioned to lead a circular bioeconomy around hemp," Walczyk said, "with farmers ready to grow, universities advancing R&D, startups producing feedstocks and products, and the nation's largest concentration of architects and builders."

Alexandros Tsamis, Director of the Troy, NY-based Center for Architecture Science & Ecology (CASE). Photo courtesy of Rensselaer Polytechnic Institute

ACADEMIC LISTINGS & TESTING AGENCIES

■ Lawrence, Mike. University of Bath, UK. - "Moisture Buffer Potential of Experimental Wall Assemblies Incorporating Formulated Hemp-lime" 2015 Building and Environment

■ Maguire, Marc. Durham School of Architectural Engineering and Construction, University of Nebraska, Lincoln. Research on hemp-based concrete. marc.maguire@unl.edu

■ Magwood, Chris. Builders for Climate Action. chris@chrismagwood.ca - "Achieving Real Net-Zero Emission Homes: Embodied carbon scenario analysis of the upper tiers of performance in the 2020 Canadian National Building Code." 2021 Natural Resources Canada/Builders for Climate Action

■ Martínez, Borja. Polytechnic University of Catalonia, Terrassa, Spain. Department of Strength of Materials and Structures in Engineering. borja.martinez@upc.edu. "Applications and Properties of Hemp Stalk-Based Insulating Biomaterials for Buildings: Review" April, 2023 Materials (Basil)

■ McDonald, Armando. University of Idaho. armandm@uidaho.edu - Determining the R-Value of bast hemp fiber insulation batts (ongoing research)

■ McPhail, Leeland. Rhode Island School of Design School of Architecturelmcphail@risd.edu

■ Memari, Ali. Pennsylvania State University. College of

Students apply hemp lime to forms in the walls of the K-State Casita, a traveling hemp structure meant to show off building materials. Photo courtesy of Michael Gibson.

Engineering. Pennsylvania Housing Research Center. amm7@psu.edu. "Thermal, Energy, and Indoor Environmental Quality Performance of the PA Hemp House" 2022.

■ Milagros Rivas Aybar, Daniela, Curtin University, Perth, Australia, Sustainable Engineering Group, School of Civil and Mechanical Engineering. d.rivasaybar@postgrad.curtin.edu.au. "Enhancing eco-efficiency in hemp-based construction boards: environmental and economic strategies for sustainability"July 2024 Australasian Journal of Environmental Management

■ Muhit, Imrose B. Teesside University, School of Computing, Engineering & Digital Technologies i.muhit@tees.ac.uk. "A holistic sustainability overview of hemp as building and highway construction materials." May, 2024 Building and Environment

■ Oti, Jonathon E. University of South Wales, UK. jonathan.oti@southwales.ac.uk "The Development of Stabilised Clay-Hemp Building Material for Sustainability and Low Carbon Use" 2020, Journal of Civil Engineering and Construction

ACADEMIC LISTINGS & TESTING AGENCIES

■ Page, Jonathon. University d'Artois, France.jonathan.page@univ-artois.fr - "Design and multi-physical properties of a new hybrid hemp-flax composite material" 2017 Construction and Building Materials

■ Piątkiewicz, Wojciech. Faculty of Civil Engineering, Warsaw University of Technology. wojciech.piatkiewicz.dokt@pw.edu.pl "Determination of Compressive Strength in Hemp–Lime Composites: Comparative Study ..." 2026 Applied Sciences

■ Pietruszka, B. Building Research Institute, Warsaw. b.pietruszka@itb.pl "Characterization of Hemp-Lime Bio-Composite" 2019 IOP Conference Series: Earth and Environmental Science

■ Pochwała, Sławomir. Opole University of Technology, Poland. s.pochwala@po.edu.pl - "The Heat Conductivity Properties of Hemp–Lime Composite Material Used in Single-Family Buildings", 2020, Materials

■ Ruth, Jonsara & Mears, Alison. ruthj@newschool.edu, mearsa@newschool.edu Parsons New School Healthy Materials Lab, NYC, NY. Resources: Hemp & Lime. 2022

■ Shareef, Sardar S. Tishk International University-Sulaimani, Iraq. Architectural Engineering Department,. Faculty of Engineering. "Using Hemp for Walls as a Sustainable Building Material" 2022 Journal of Studies in Science and Engineering.

■ Sideris, Petros. Texas A & M University. petros.sideris@tamu.edu Study of hempcrete for 3D printing. Ongoing research 2023

■ Shea, Andy. University of Bath, UK.a.shea@bath.ac.uk - "Hygrothermal performance of an experimental hemp–lime building" 2012, Construction and Building Materials

■ Strandberg-de Bruijn, Paulien. Lund University, Sweden. paulien.strandberg@byggtek.lth.se "Full-scale Studies of Improving Energy Performance by Renovating Historic Swedish Timber Buildings with Hemp-lime" 2019 Applied Sciences

■ Tsamis, Alexandros & Walczyk, Daniel. Rensselaer Polytechnic Institute CASE Center for Architecture, Science and Ecology, NY. tsamia@rpi.edu, walczd@rpi.edu. Dept. of Energy-funded research for HeRs hemp insulation and hemp-based rebar. 2023

■ Tucker, Simon. Liverpool John Moores University, UK.s.s.tucker@ljmu.ac.uk - "Quasi steady state and dynamic hygrothermal performance of fibrous Hemp and Stone Wool insulations: Two innovative laboratory based investigations" 2016 Building and Environment

■ Ulven, Chad, et al. North Dakota State University Dept. of Mechanical Engineering. Chad.Ulven@ndsu.edu. Ongoing research on hurd sizing for building grade standards.

Sergiy 'Doctor Hemphouse' Kovalenkov conducts a chilrdren hempcrete workshop in Ashland, OR. Photo courtesy of Sergiy Kovalenkov.

ACADEMIC LISTINGS & TESTING AGENCIES

■ Walker, R. Trinity College, Dublin, Ireland. walkerro@tcd.ie - "Moisture transfer and thermal properties of hemp–lime concretes," 2014 Construction Building Materials.

■ Yazdanseta, Arta. School of Architecture, Rensselaer Polytechnic Institute. yazdaa@rpi.edu "Knowledge Mapping for Advancement of Hemp-Lime Composite in the Construction Industry: A Systematic Literature Review (2004–2024)" Open Access Study.

■ Zhang, Yakun, et al. Oregon State University, Department of Crop and Soil Science. yakun.zhang@oregonstate.edu "Utilizing agricultural and forest residue for 3D printing of cement-free infrastructure."

Kansas Hempcrete Casita built by KSU students and Stuc-Go-Crete. Photo courtesy of Kristin Santorelli.

TESTING AGENCIES

The following testing and R & D services have tested Hemp-lime for ASTM standards

RD SERVICES - *Watertown, TN*
Thermal Insulation testing ASTM C-118
rdservices.com

WESTERN FIRE CENTER - *Kelso, WA*
Ignition resistance ASTM E-119
Westernfire.com

INTERTEK - *Multiple locations (international)*
ASTM testing
Intertek.com

CHAPTER 6

INTERNATIONAL HEMP BUILDERS & SUPPLIERS

INTERNATIONAL LISTINGS

AUSTRALIA

NSW

ASHFORD HEMP INDUSTRIES PTY LTD
- *Ashford NSW*
Hemp Hurd (Shiv) Provider
Contact: Connie Minos
Ashfordhempindustries.com

AUSTRALIA HEMP MASONRY PTY LTD.
- *Lismore NSW*
Training Provider, Lime binder supplies
Contact: Klara Marosszeky
Hempmasonry.com.au

BALANCED EARTH ARCHITECTS
- *Wilsons Creek NSW*
Architect/Designer
Contact: Michael Leung
Balancedeartharchitects.com

BALANCED EARTH BUILDERS PTY
- *Mullumbimby NSW*
Green Builder, Hempcrete Installer
Contact: Luke Wrencher
Balancedearth.co

BELUBULA HEMP HOMES
- *Canowindra NSW*
Green Builder, Hempcrete Installer
Contact: James Isaacs
Belubula.au

BHI BUILDERS
- *Old Bar NSW*
Green Builder
Contact: Mitch Brown
Bhibuilders.com.au

CONNECTED DESIGN
- *Marrickville NSW*
Architect/Designer
Contact: Tracy Graham
Connecteddesign.com.au

ECO DYNAMIC BUILDING
- *Coffs Harbour NSW*
Green Builder, Hempcrete Installer
Contact: Luke McKay
Ecodynamicbuilding.com.au

EMILY KNIGHT DESIGN
- *Ashbury NSW*
Architect
Contact: Emily Knight
Ekd.com.au

ENVIRONMENTARIAN
- *Sydney NSW*
Architecture/Design
Contact: Jeremy Thomas
Environmentarian.au

ENVIROTECTURE
- *Ballarat NSW*
Architecture
Contact: Talina Edwards
Envirotecture.com.au

GREEN E BUILDING
Green Builder, Hempcrete Installer
Contact: Adrian Medcraft
Green-e-building.com

HEMP LIME CO
- *Stockton NSW*
Hemp Hurd (Shiv) Provider, Hempcrete Installer, Lime/binder Provider, Training Provider
Contact: Hudson Doyle
Hemplime.com.au

HEMP PROCESSING AUSTRALIA
- *Darlinghurst NSW*
Hemp Processor, Hemp Hurd (Shiv) Provider
Contact: Anthony Coffey
Hempprocessingaust.com.au

Australian Hempcrete Passive House Coliving Home in Central Victoria. Photo courtesy Dan Prohaska.

INTERNATIONAL LISTINGS

Hempcrete home on the Sunshine Coast, QLD. Photo courtesy of Ecolibrium Designs.

MOORHOUSE CONSTRUCTIONS
- Mannering Park NSW
Green Builder, Hempcrete Installer
Contact: Michael Lancaster
Moorhouseconstructions@gmail.com

MY BUILDING CERTIFIER
- Kirrawee NSW
Architect/Engineer
Contact: Rhys Hood
Mybuildingcertifier.com.au

SHELTER BUILDING DESIGN
- Hazelbrook NSW
Architect, Training Provider
Contact: Kirstie Wulf
Shelterbuildingdesign.com.au

SOILIFE GROUP PTY LTD
- South Murwillumbah NSW
Training Provider
Contact: Adam Abbott
Soilife.com.au

SOUTHERN HEMP
- Moama NSW
Hempcrete Installer
Contact: David Brian
Southernhemp.au

SOWDEN BUILDING SOLUTIONS
- Balmain NSW
Hempcrete Installer
Contact: Nick Sowden
Sowdenbuildingsolutions.com.au

TANKSPRAY *- Young NSW*
Hempcrete Installer
Contact: Peter Robinson
Tankspray.com.au

QLD
Featured
HEMPBLOCK AUSTRALIA *- Sunshine Coast, QLD*
Hemp Blocks, Architecture, Engineering
Hempblockaustralia.com
Contact: Johan Tijssen
admin@hempblockaustralia.com
61-1-300 814 834

ECOLIBRIUM DESIGNS
- Eumundi QLD
Architect/Designer
Contact: Brett Grimley
Ecolibrium.com.au

FENECH BUILDING
- Nobby Beach QLD
Green Builder, Hempcrete Installer
Contact: Clinton Fenech
Fenechbuilding.com.au

WANDARRA PTY LTD
- South Townsville QLD
Hemp Hurd (Shiv) Provider
Contact: Ramone Close
Wandarra.com.au

SA
CCBUILD *- Port Lincoln SA*
Green Builder, Hempcrete Installer
Contact: David "Cyril" Carr
Ccbuild.info

HEMP BUILDING DIRECTORY 2026

LEADER PROFILE

KLARA MAROSSZEKY
Hempcrete Performs in Australia's Climate Conditions

Australian Hemp Masonry was established in 2014 following 15 years of research. We were the first Australian hempcrete material to market, and we've maintained a heavy involvement in R&D which I've overseen, including for fire (we're flame zone rated). We've also developed alternative low carbon binders and prefab solutions.

For the last three years, we have studied performance and buildability challenges presented by Australia's diverse climatic conditions and collated comparative data on different forms of hempcrete.

We've supplied to over 250 residential projects in Australia and to 3 projects in New Zealand.

What was a win for your company in the past year?

We delivered on two very interesting and different commercial builds, a major internationally awarded project, "The Forest" at the University of Tasmania and a shop fitout for Patagonia who've taken a stand on stopping native forest logging.

Klara Marosszeky is founder and managing director of the Australian Hemp Masonry Pty Ltd., based in Lismore, NSW.

It's been challenging at times sticking to our vision to support Australian farmers rather than just buying hemp from overseas. It's slowed our growth, as small scale manufacturing is expensive but it's a no-brainer that that's what needs to happen to minimise global emissions.

Public endorsement by higher-profile Australians who understand the breadth of climate-related issues is essential, and lots more education.

> " *If people understood hempcrete's carbon storage potential, I believe they would really embrace hemp construction.* "

INTERNATIONAL LISTINGS

HARDY HEMP HOMES
- Lenswood SA
Hempcrete Installer
Contact: Madeleine Hardy
Hardyhemphomes@yahoo.com.au

SPACECRAFT DESIGN BUILD - *Newton SA*
Architect, Green Builder, Hempcrete Installer
Contact: Henry Keene
Spacecraft.net.au

TWO CREATIVE PTY LTD
-SA
Hempcrete Installer, Plasterer
Contact: Scott Goldie
Skgoldie@bigpond.com

TAS
DIRTY EARL NATURAL BUILDING - *Tasmania*
Green Builder, Hempcrete Installer
Contact: Carriane Earl Boyd
Muddymaori@gmail.com

JENNIFER BINNS DESIGN
- St Helens TAS
Architect/Designer
Contact: Jennifer Binns
Jenniferbinnsdesign.com.au

X-HEMP PTY LTD
- Cressy TAS
Hemp Processor
Contact: Andi Lucas
X-hemp.au

VIC
ALTERECO DESIGN
- Anglesea VIC
Architect/Designer
Contact: James Goodlet
Altereco.net.au

BREATHE - *Melbourne*
Contact: Joost Bakker
Breathe.com.au

ENVIROTECTURE
- Ballarat VIC
Architecture/Designer
Contact: Andy Marlow
Envirotecture.com.au

HEMPCRETE AUSTRALIA
- Frankston VIC
Green Builder, Hempcrete Installer, Hemp hurd (shiv) provider
Contact: Mathieu Gervais
Hempcrete.com.au

HEMPCRETE INSTALLATION
- Welshmans Reef VIC
Hempcrete Installer
Contact: Andy Liepins
Hempcrete.construction@gmail.com

HEMPCRETE VICTORIA
- Melbourne VIC
Green Builder, Hempcrete Installer, Training Provider
Contact: Will Brain
Hempcretevictoria.com.au

THE HEMP BUILDING COMPANY AUSTRALIA
- Kyneton VIC
Green Builder, Hempcrete Installer, Plaster
Contact: Joe D'Alo
Thehempbuildingcompany.com.au

NEGATIVE CARBON LIVING
- Frankston South VIC
Green Builder, Hempcrete Installer
Contact: Dale King
Ncliving.com.au

HempBLOCK home in Australia. Photo courtesy of HempBLOCK International.

INTERNATIONAL LISTINGS

PETE COLLINGS ARCHITECT
- *Stratford VIC*
Architect/Designer
Contact: Pete Collings
Petecollingsarchitect.wordpress.com

PRO HEMP
- *Pakenham, VIC*
Hemp hurd (shiv) provider
Contact: Matthew Box
Prohemp.com.au

RESPIRA BUILT
- *Coburg North VIC*
Hemp Blocks
Contact: Will Brain
Respirabuilt.com.au
Hempcretevictoria.com.au

STEFFEN WELSCH ARCHITECTS
- *Collingwood VIC*
Architect/Designer
Contact: Steffen Welsch
Steffenwelsch.com.au

WA

ANDREW HUGHES DRAFTING AND DESIGN
- *Denmark WA*
Architect/Designer
Contact: Andrew Hughes
Ahughesdrafting@gmail.com

HEMP ENGINEERING PTY. - *Perth WA*
Engineer
Contact: Ramon Granados
Hempengineering.com.au

HEMP HOMES AUSTRALIA
- *Margaret River, WA*
Green Builder, Hemp Hurd (Shiv) Provider, Hempcrete Installer
Contact: Gary Rogers
Hemphomesaustralia.net.au

HEMP SQUARED PTY.
- *Bridgetown, WA*
Hemp Blocks
Contact: Iggy Van
Hemp-squared.com.au

HOMES BY NATURE
- *Witchcliffe, WA*
Green Builder, Hempcrete Installer
Contact: Cameron Richardson
Homesbynature.com.au

MIRRECO - *Perth WA*
Engineer, Hemp Building Materials Supplier, Researcher
Contact: Rich Evans
Mirreco.com

NEW EARTH LIVING
- *Forest Grove WA*
Contact: Brendan Kelly
Newearthliving.com.au

OZHEMP - *Kardinya, WA*
Hemp Hurd (Shiv) Provider, Lime Binder Provider
Contact: Donald Khoo
Ozhemp.com.au

WITCHCLIFFE ECOVILLAGE - *Witchcliffe, WA*
Green Builder, Hempcrete Installer
Ecovillage.net.au

Hempcrete Home on PhilipIsland, VIC. Photo-courtesy-of-Real-Estate.com.au.

INTERNATIONAL LISTINGS

AUSTRIA

ARCHITEKTUR-BAU-MEISTER — BISCHOF I ZÜNDEL - *Lingenau*
Contact: Laurin Zündel, Stephan Bischof
Bischof-zuendel.at

HEMPSTATIC GMBH - *Vienna*
Acoustic Panels
Contact: Elena Yaneva
Hempstatic.at

NAPORO KLIMA DÄMMSTOFF GMBH (STRABAG) - *Haugsdorf*
Contact: Klemens Haselsteiner
Naporo.com

BELGIUM

AXEL VERVOORDT - *Wijnegem*
Architect
Axel-vervoordt.com

C-BIOTEC - *Temse*
Hemp building materials
Contact: Ingmar Nopens
C-biotech.eu

CREATIVE TECHNICAL SOLUTIONS - *Gullegem*
Engineer; Equipment Sales, Rental
Contact: Stefaan Declerck
Cretes.be

ECOMAT - *Zandhoven*
Insulation Batts; Hemp Blocks
Contact: Rudi Ghelen
Ecomat.be

EXIE NV - *Herzele*
Contact: Mathieu Hendrickx
Exie.be

HERMELIJN - *Leuvensesteenweg*
Contact: Peter Callewaert
Lime/binder Provider; Hemp Blocks
Ecologischebouwmaterialen.be

HET LEEMNISCAAT - *Zoersel*
Green Builder; Hempcrete Installer; Architect
Hetleemniscaat.be

ISOHEMP - *Fernelmont*
Hemp Blocks
Contact: Gaëtan Dujardin
Isohemp.com

HYLER - *West-flandres*
Engineer; Hemp Processing Technology
Contact: Niels Baert
Hyler.be

MVC ARCHITECTEN - *Gent*
Architect; Engineer
Contact: Robbe Van Caimere
Mvc-architecten.be

OTRA CONSTRUCTION - *Wavre*
Hemp Blocks; Plaster; Hempcrete Installer; Green Builder
Contact: Laurent Ruidant
Otra.be

VERHELST GROEP - *Oudenburg*
Hemp Blocks
Contact: Kathleen Verhelst
Verhelst.be

WOONDER CVBA - *Gent*
Green Builder; Educational Institution; Hempcrete Installer
Contact: Hilde Vanwildemeersch
Woonderbouw.be

BULGARIA

HEMPCRETE BULGARIA - *Yugozapaden*
Green Builder; Hempcrete Installer
Contact: Dimitar Mihaylov
Konopobeton.bg

Hempcrete insulated natural materials facility in Austria. Photo courtesy Nussbaumer photography.

LEADER PROFILE
GAËTAN DUJARDIN
Hemp Blocks Redefine Building Performance and Comfort

Hemp-based materials do not only address environmental challenges; they also solve issues that are often poorly covered by conventional construction methods, such as summer thermal comfort and acoustic comfort. We are not just reducing the environmental impact of construction — we are going beyond it and redefining building performance and comfort.

What was a win for your company in the past year?

IsoHemp focuses on quality and on adapting to the demanding standards of mature construction markets. Our products are specified in increasingly ambitious projects, including multi-story buildings, which clearly demonstrates the growing credibility and technical maturity of hemp construction.

What is something about hemp building/construction/processing you didn't know a year ago?

What has become even more evident over the past year is the significant impact of hemp construction on summer comfort and energy savings during heat waves. This aspect is increasingly mentioned by designers and clients and has clearly emerged as one of the strongest differentiating factors compared to conventional construction solutions.

The market often focuses on only part of the equation — for example thermal performance alone — or relies on habits deeply rooted in conventional construction, such as the belief that a building must be completely airtight. The solution lies in a constructive and continuous educational approach toward all market stakeholders. This requires a major effort in simplification, popularization, and appropriation of technical concepts, so that architects, engineers, and contractors can fully understand, trust, and ultimately change their mindset toward hemp-based construction.

Gaëtan Dujardin is export sales manager at IsoHemp, based in Fernelmont, Belgium.

INTERNATIONAL LISTINGS

CANADA

CANADIAN HEMP TRADE ASSN. - *Calgary, AB*
Education, Training Provider
Hemptrade.ca

AB

3D SPACE TERRAFORM
- *Wabamun AB*
Engineer
Contact: Christina Goodvin
3dspaceterraform.com

8TH FIRE INNOVATIONS /DIVITA BLOCKS
- *Edmonton, AB*
Green Builder; Hempcrete Installer; Hemp Blocks
Contact: Dion Lefebvre
8thfireinnovations.com

HEMP CARBON STANDARD - *Calgary*
Financial Services
Contact: Tim de Rosen
Hempcarbonstandard.org

LEGACY FIBERS
- *Coronation*
Contact: Matthew Hanger
Hemp Processor
Legacyfibers.ca

TERRAFIBRE
- *Drayton* Valley AB
Contact: Troy White
Insulation Batts
Terrafibre.ca

WELLWOOD MASTER BUILDER
- *Edmonton AB*
Green Builder
Contact: Derek Lammie
Wellwoodmasterbuilt.com

BC

Featured
SILACOTE CANADA
- *Williams Lake BC*
Contact: Bill Jensen
bill@silacote.com
250-770-0064

Featured
RENEWABUILD
- *Surrey*
Hemp Blocks
Contact: David Geertz
David@Renewabuild.ca
Renewabuild.ca

ALTITUDE CARPENTRY
- *Cherryville BC*
Green Builder
Contact: Rory Lalonde
Altitudecarpentry.ca

BAST FIBRE TECHNOLOGY
- *Victoria BC*
Hemp Materials
Contact: Jim Posa
Bastfibretech.com

CALMURA NATURAL WALLS INC.
- *Vancouver, BC*
Engineer; Green Builder; Researcher/Developer; Hemp Panels
Contact: Monty Chong-Walden
Calmura.ca

HEMPOWER - *Langley BC*
Hemp Hurd (shives) Provider
Contact: Patrick Harrap
Hempower.ca

CHANGE AGRONOMY
- *Manitoba BC*
Hemp processor
Contact: Mitch Rushton
Changeag.com

FOREVER GREEN INDUSTRIAL HEMP PROJECTS
- *Vanderhoof BC*
Equipment Sales/Rental
Contact: Peter Düshop
Getforevergreen.com

Hempcrete hair salon Salt Springs Island, BC, Canada. Photo courtesy of Lillian Clarke.

INTERNATIONAL LISTINGS

IsoHemp factory in Fernelmont, Belgium. Photo courtesy IsoHemp.

GREENPLAN
- *Nanaimo BC*
Architect
Contact: Jack Anderson
Greenplan.ca

HAYWOOD DESIGN
- *Penticton BC*
Architect/Designer
Contact: Jamie Miller-Haywood
Haywooddesignstudio.com

HEMP HOMES CANADA
- *Vancouver*
Contact: Tim Murphy
Hempcretehomes.ca

HEMPCRETE NATURAL BUILDING
- *Bowen Island BC*
Green Builder; Hempcrete Installer
Contact: Kim Brooks
Hempcrete.ca

INCA RENEW TECH
-*Kelowna*
Hemp batt insulation, hemp panels
Contact: David Saltman
Incarenewtech.com

RELOAD SUSTAINABLE DESIGN - *Vancouver*
Architect
Contact: Martina Soderlund
Reloadsustainable.com

ROBYN FENTON ARCHITECT
- *North Vancouver BC*
Architect/Designer
Robynfenton.ca

NB

RISE BUILDING MATERIALS - *Fredericton*
Hemp batt insulation
Contact: Matt Daigle
Buildwithrise.com

MB

ELM NATURAL BUILDERS LTD. - *Winnipeg MB*
Contact: Francesco Zurzolo
Elmnaturalbuilders.com

ON

BOSK DESIGN INC.
- *Waterloo, ON*
Architect
Contact: Rick O'Brien
Rick.obrien@rogers.com

BUILDERS FOR CLIMATE ACTION
- *Peterborough ON*
Training Provider, Researcher
Contact: Chris Magwood
Buildersforclimateaction.org

CHRISTOPHER Z. TWORKOWSKI ARCHITECT - *Lake Field ON*
Architect/Designer
Contact: Christopher Tworkowski
Christopherztworkowskiarchitect.weebly.com

DRIFTSCAPE - *Waterloo*
Architect
Contact: Chloe Doesburg
Driftscape.com

HA/F CLIMATE DESIGN
- *Toronto*
Contact: Ryan Bruer
Halfclimatedesign.com

THE HIVE DESIGN CO.
- *Kitchener-Waterloo ON*
Architect
Contact: Justine Nigro
Thehivedesignco.com

LEADER PROFILE

DAVID GEERTZ
Hemp can Scale to Match Legacy Building Products

What excites me most about hemp and bioconstruction is that it turns farmers into the new gravel pits—supplying an unlimited, renewable feedstock for the masonry industry. By creating renewable masonry, we introduce real competition to dimensional lumber, reducing pressure on forests while strengthening rural economies.

What was a win for your company in the past year?

- A major win for us this past year was completing the commercialization of our first factory and hitting our production target of two blocks per minute. We also entered into our first U.S. partnership agreement - proving that renewable masonry can scale operationally and cross borders. We see 2026 as a turning point where the U.S. begins investing heavily in bioconstruction.

What bottlenecks have you observed in the industrial hemp industry and how would you solve them?

The biggest bottleneck in the natural building industry is permitting speed. Alternative materials often get stuck in long approval cycles because regulators rely on prescriptive codes written for conventional products. We solve this by using engineering-grade simulation tools like FEA and ANSYS to generate defensible performance data, Structural, fire, thermal, and durability, before a shovel hits the ground. Once permitting friction is removed, natural materials like hemp can scale quickly and compete on equal footing with legacy construction products.

David Geertz is founder and business development leader at Renewabuild, based in Surrey, BC, Canada.

> " What excites me most about hemp and bioconstruction is that it turns farmers into the new gravel pits—supplying an unlimited, renewable feedstock for the masonry industry. "

INTERNATIONAL LISTINGS

ZON ENGINEERING
- *Guelph ON*
Engineer
Contact: Jordan Hoogendam
Zonengineering.com

QC

ARTCAN - *Quebec, QC*
Green Builder; Hempcrete Installer; Hemp Blocks
Contact: Gabriel Gauthier
Maisonenchanvre.com

ART DU CHANVRE
- *Quebec, QC*
Green Builder; Hempcrete Installer; Training Provider
Contact: Anthony Néron
Duchanvre.com

HECO INNOVATION CHANVRE INC
- *Quebec QC*
Engineer, Research & Development, Hemp insulation batts
Contact: Philippe Fortin
Heco-innovation.com

NATURE FIBRES, INC.
- *Val des Sources QC*
Hemp Batt Insulation, Hemp Building Materials
Contact: Christiane Bérubé
Naturefibres.com/en/

NOVENVIRO INC
- *Cowansville*
Lime/binder Provider, Hemp Hurd (Shiv) Provider, Hemp Blocks, Insulation Batts, Plaster, Resin/Paints/Stains
Contact: Nicolas Seguin
Novenviro.com/en

COSTA RICA

CJI GROUP - *Costa Rica*
Green Builder, Architect/Designer
Contact: Jack Geier
Thecjigroup.com

ZEGREENLAB - *Lorena*
Green Builder
Contact: Ashley Javogue
Zegreenlab.com/en

CYPRESS

2050 MATERIALS
- *Limassol*
Hemp Materials Supplier
Contact: Phanos Hadjikyriakou
2050-materials.com

CZECH REPUBLIC

MABEKO – *Svor*
Green Builder, Hempcrete Installer
Contact: Jan Bešík
Mabeko.cz

NORICUM - *Bubeneč*
Green Builder; Hemp Hurd (Shiv) Provider; Lime/binder Provider; Training Provider; Resin/Paints/Stains
Konopny-beton.cz

Hempcrete greenhouse, Berneck, Switzerland built by Toni Laderach Hemp Eco System. Photo courtesy of Lillian Clarke.

Restoring the Ruined Portugal Village of Chumbaria with Hemp

By Sarah McGuinness

The village of Chumbaria is being lovingly restored by a UK couple using hempcrete blocks. Photo courtesy of Sarah McGuinniss

When my husband, Steve, and I moved from the UK to Portugal's Silver Coast, we certainly didn't plan on buying an entire ruined village. Our original idea was just a small house and an Airbnb conversion. But then Chumbaria caught my eye online—it was love at first sight! We bought the small cluster of derelict stone buildings for €200,000, and our epic renovation journey began.

Our goal was simple: bring this historic space back to life while prioritizing sustainability and honoring the buildings' past.

We've now completed Phase 1, transforming two old barns into unique, luxurious guest accommodations. Originally, these thick-walled stone structures served utilitarian purposes—storing olive oil, grain, and housing oxen. Now, they're holiday rentals, but the challenge was insulation and modernization.

We proudly worked with local builders and tradesmen but the biggest innovation was incorporating hempcrete blocks from Alentejo-based supplier Canhamor.

The renovation process preserved the original stone walls, securing them with a concrete ring beam. We left a 5 cm air gap between the old stone and the new hemp blocks. This allows the hemp to "breathe naturally," as well as providing a discrete space for installing wiring and pipes. While our initial plan was a smooth lime render, we changed our minds.

Once we saw the natural beauty of the hemp blocks, we decided to leave them exposed, highlighting the sustainable materials and craftsmanship. The rustic look is sympathetic to the building's original purpose.

The Hempcrete Difference: Function and Feel
We are absolutely delighted with the hempcrete blocks. The difference they've made is remarkable.

The results of using hempcrete have been remarkable, both functionally and for the guest experience.

The material has solved the common issues of dampness and drafts found in old stone buildings. No matter what the weather outside, inside both houses are warm in the winter, cool in the summer, very dry and very quiet.

But it's the atmosphere the hempcrete creates that guests love most. Beyond the acoustic properties and year-round comfort, visitors appreciate the tranquility. Many have described the feeling of being inside as the buildings giving them a "hug."

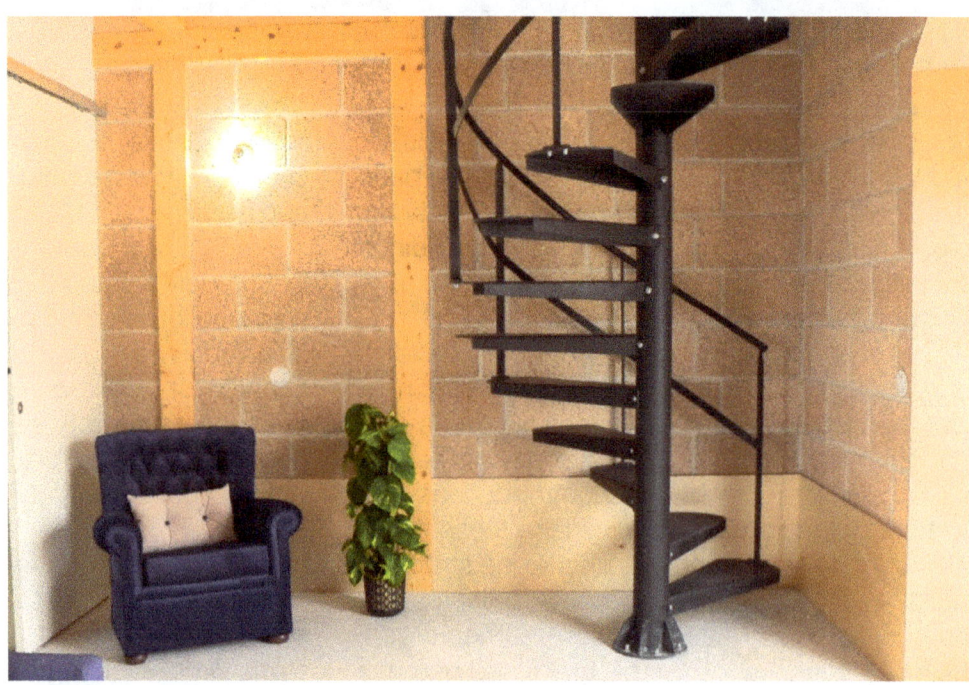

The former barns have been remodeled into a stylish holiday rental. Photo courtesy of Sarah McGuinness

The quality of the construction and the commitment to sustainable materials haven't gone unnoticed. We were incredibly proud that our hempcrete houses were nominated for Building of the Year in Archdaily!

Since opening in 2024, our two properties have hosted over 400 guests, and we've achieved Superhost status on Airbnb. The unique hemp construction is a major talking point for us.

We have had many guests who have come to stay out of curiosity, which has increased our revenue considerably.

Hempcrete blocks delivered. Photo courtesy of Sarah McGuinness.

The success of Phase 1 has cemented our plans for the future. Having witnessed the remarkable benefits first hand, we are thrilled to announce that all eight of our remaining village houses will also be restored using hempcrete blocks.

Plastered and remodeled holiday rental insulated with hempcrete blocks. Photo courtesy of Sarah McGuinness

LEADER PROFILE

INGMAR NOPENS
Win-Win – Hemp can Decarbonize Construction and Heal the Soil

I oversee all the activities of the company covering the value chain of industrial hemp from seed to construction material, including growing hemp on PFAS contaminated soil.

We provide holistic solutions capturing carbon, cleaning polluted soils and providing bio-based materials for a circular economy.

Using hemp as a soil remediator and decarboniser of the construction sector. A win-win.

What was a win for your company in the past year?

We opened our first hemp insulation batt factory in Germany in a partnership with Hempflax.

What we learned:

Weather conditions are even more important regarding the quality of the product than we had anticipated.

The industry is still very fragmented. Setting up strong partnerships is key to unlock the industry.

Ingmar Nopens is managing director of C-Biotech, based in Temse, Belgium.

> " *Using hemp as a soil remediator and decarboniser of the construction sector. A win-win.* "

INTERNATIONAL LISTINGS

DENMARK

BUILDING TOMORROW
- Horsens
Green Builder
Contact: Darius Moravcik
Buildingtomorrow.dk

HAMPENS HUS
- Nykøbing Falster
Contact: Jonas Aarsø
Bioguldborgsund.dk

HAVNENS HÆNDER
- København
Contact: Mikkel Damgaard Nielsen
Havnens-h.dk

HENNING-LARSEN
- Copenhagen
Architect
Contact: Martha Lewis
Henninglarsen.com/en

ESTONIA

UKU PURE EARTH
- Põlva maakond
Plaster, Lime/binder Provider
Contact: Marko Kikas
Uku.eu

Apartment building with 92 social housing units built in Villeurbanne, France with BioSys blocks by Groupe Mazaud. Photo courtesy of Groupe Mazaud.

INTERNATIONAL LISTINGS

FRANCE

Educational Institutions/Training Providers

L'ACADÉMIE DES BIOSOURCÉS - *Pornic*
Contact: Quentin Pichon
Academiedesbiosources.fr

BDE THERMAIR - *Bruyere*
Contact: Cedric Rosa
Thermair.fr

BTP CFA - *Ocquerre*
Contact: Severine Guyon
Atpcfa-iledefrance.fr

CONSTRUIRE EN CHANVRE - *Paris*
Contact: Daniel Daviller
Construire-en-chanvre.fr/informations

DOMO SAPIENS - *Le Puy en Valay*
Contact: Didier Bayoud
Domo-sapiens.fr

ENTPE - *Vaulx-en-Velin*
Contact: Cécile Delolme
Entpe.fr

L'ÉCOLE NATIONALE DU CHANVRE - *Mende*
Contact: Max Scholtes
Ecolenationaleduchanvre.com

MFR RIAILLÉ - *Riaillé*
Contact: Vincent Corbard
Mfr-riaille.com

SARL SOLENER - *Lille*
Contact: Mohamed Abdesselam
Solener.fr

SOCIÉTÉ INNOVANTE DE CONSTRUCTION EN CHANVRE (SI2C) - *Mézière*
Contact: Gérard Lenain

TRIBU - *Paris*
Contact: Edith Akiki
Tribu-concevoirdurable.fr

Hempcrete 19 unit apartment building in Widnau, Switzerland. Photo courtesy of Openly.

LEADER PROFILE

XAVIER DELACOUR

Demand and Interest for Hemp Blocks Production is Increasing in the World

We are, as equipment manufacturers, following the development and inquiries of our customers and the new tendencies in biosourced building material.

What was a win for your company in the past year?

To sell production plants to make Hemp blocks to companies CANHAMOR in Portugal, ISOHEMP in Belgium and VIEILLE in France. The demand and interest for hemp blocks production is increasing in the world.

What bottlenecks have you observed in the industrial hemp industry and how would you solve them?

This industry needs to be structured and organized in order to compete better compared to other building material industries like concrete.

> "This industry needs to be structured and organized in order to compete better compared to other building material industries..."

Xavier Delacour is the export sales director of France- and US-based Quadra Concrete, manufacturing robotic-assisted block-making machinery

INTERNATIONAL LISTINGS

Architect/Engineer

JULIEN AUBESSARD ARCHITECTE - *Lyon*
Architect; Engineer

JA-ARCHITECTE.FR ADBPA SARL D'ARCHITECT - *Paris*
Architect
Contact: A. Brochard
Abdpa.com

AGEXEA - *Rosny sous Bois*
Architect; Engineer
Contact: Mohamed Ali Adala
Agexea.com

ANATOMIES D'ARCHITECTURE - *Paris*
Contact: Mathis Rager
Anatomiesdarchitecture.com

ARIETUR ATELIER D'ARCHITECTURE - *Wimille*
Architect
Contact: Christine Cacheux
Arietur.com

ARP-ASTRANCE - *Paris*
Architect; Engineer
Contact: Xavier Lassudrie Duchene
Arp-astrance.com

ARCHITECTURE RÉGÉN-ÉRATIVE SARL - *Paris*
Architect
Architecture-regenerative.com
Contact: Vanessa Grob

SIDONIE BOËHM ARCHITECTE - *Chambéry*
Mail@sidonieboehm.com

ATELIER BELENFANT DAUBAS - *Nozay*
Architect
Contact: Mélanie Perrichet
Atelierbelenfantdaubas.org

ATELIER WOA - *Paris*
Architect
Contact: Samuel Poutoux
Atelier-woa.fr

BARRAULT PRESSACCO - *Paris*
Architect
Contact: Thibaut Barrault
Barraultpressacco.com

BELUS & HENOCQ ARCHITECTES - *Paris*
Architect
Contact: Guillaume Belus
Belushenocq.fr

BN ARCHITECTURES - *Meaux*
Architect
Contact: Olivier Neyraud
Bn-architectures.com

CAN INGEINEURS-ARCHTECTES - *Reze*
Architect; Engineer
Contact: Margaux Petillon
Can-ia.fr

DUMONT LEGRAND ARCHITECTES - *Paris*
Architect
Contact: Olivier Legrand
Dumont-legrand.fr

ATELIER EMILIE DUPUY ARCHITECTE - *Vertou*
Emiliedupuy@yahoo.fr

ATELIER GROSS - *Orbey*
Contact: Jean-Francois Gross
Gross.jfrancois@gmail.com

Hemp home in Lithuania constructed by Hempbalt. Courtesy of Juozas Jankauskas.

INTERNATIONAL LISTINGS

Menorca hempcrete ecological hotel Son Blanc. Photo courtesy Atelier du Pont Architectes.

XAVIER JOUSSE ARCHITECTE
- *Issy les Moulineaux*
Xavierjousse@gmail.com

LEMOAL LEMOAL ARCHITECTES - *Paris*
Architect
Contact: Christophe Lemoal
Lemoal-lemoal.com

LM INGÉNIERIE
- *Haguenau*
Engineer
Contact: Laurent Mouly
lm-ingenierie.fr

M'CUB ARCHITECTES
- *Montreuil*
Architect
Contact: Christian Hackel
Mcub.eu

MEDITRAG
- *Saint-Thibéry*
Engineer
Meditrag.fr

ESTELLE MIGNOT
- *Villespassans*
Architect
Estelle.mignot@hotmail.fr

MIR ARCHITECTES
- *Paris*
Architect
Contact: Nicolas Gaudard
Mirarchitectes.fr

ATELIER MONJAUZE ARCHITECTES
- *Le Puy en Velay*
Architect
Contact: Rudy Ricciotti
Eco-architecte.com

NORTH BY NORTHWEST ARCHITECTES - *Paris*
Architect
Contact: Christine Desert
Nxnw.fr

SOA ARCHITECTES
- *Paris*
Architect
Contact: Augustin Rosenstiehl
Soa-architectes.fr

TRACES À BÂTIR - *Paris*
Architect
Contact: Laura Nagapin
Tracesabatir.fr

ZEFCO - *Paris*
Architect; Engineer
Contact: François Peyron
Zefco.fr

INTERNATIONAL LISTINGS

Green Builder/ Hempcrete Installer

2K-KONCEPT
- *Villemur sur Tarn*
Contact: Lionel Decemps
2k-koncept.fr

ACOUSTIQUE AGNA
- *Clermont-Ferrand*
Contact: Nicolas Lounis
Acoustique-agna.fr

AJILIT - *Villeveque*
Contact: Nicolas Consigny
Ajilit.sarl@orange.fr

SARL AFFINIS - *Brittany*
Contact: Gautier Le Tumelin
+33 06 31 72 02 92

ARTISAN DE LA PIERRE
- *Montpeyroux*
Contact: Jean Michel Moisset
Artisan2lapierre@gmail.com

ARTPEGE RÉNOVATION
- *Laroque Timbaut*
Contact: Benoît Quentin
Artpege.fr

ASSISE CONSTRUCTION - *Bordeaux*
Contact: Leonard De Lamarliere
Assise.fr

L'AUTRE MAISON
- *Uzeste*
Contact: Jean-Pascal Despaux
Despaux1@outlook.fr

AUX CHARPENTIERS DE FRANCE
- *Villebon sur Yvette*
Contact: Bernard Delaunay
Charpentiersdefrance.com

AVENIR ET BÂTI
- *Saint Pierre D'Albigny*
Contact: Nicolas Barbier
Nicolas.barbier.pro@gmail.com

STEPHANE BARRIOL
- *Saint Germain de Calberte*
Stephanebarriol48@gmail.com

SARL BATIPLATRE PROVENCE - *St Maximin la Ste Baume*
Contact: Dany D'Angelo
Batiplatreprovence-var.fr

BATI'RENOV
- *Les Maillys*
Contact: Ludovic Poissenot
Bat-renov.com

LE BATIMENT ASSOCIE
- *Muizon*
Contact: Christophe Posseme
Batiment-associe.fr

BRÉGÉ SA
- *Le Malesherbois*
Contact: Francis Barres

OLIVIER BLANC
- *Vebron*
Olivier.blanc48@orange.fr

BOIS ET TOITS SAS
- *Villenoy*
Contact: Yvan Dudzicki
Bois-et-toits.com

SARL BOUSIGES CRÉATIONS
- *Mouans-Sartoux*
Bousiges-creations.com

SÉBASTIEN BOUARD
- *Brouzet les Ales*
Sebastien.bouard@neuf.fr

BURIN PENET
- *Boissy-le-Châtel*
Contact: Roger Penet
Burin-penet.fr

SARL S E E BURG
- *Saint Projet*
Contact: Dominique Burg
Burg-construction.com

CALYCLAY - *Le Goubet*
Contact: Noé Solsona
Calyclay.com

Hemp build in Savoie France. Photo courtesy of Greendom.

LEADER PROFILE

DANIEL DAVILLER
Growth of Hemp-Lime Represents a Shift in Philosophy

I am a technical leader and recognized expert in hemp-based construction and bio-based building materials. I have been deeply involved in the structuring, scaling, and technical validation of hemp concrete systems in France and internationally. As president of "Construire en Chanvre", the French professional association dedicated to hemp concrete, I contribute to structuring the sector, supporting standards and certifications, training professionals, and promoting best practices across the entire value chain.

What most interests me about hemp and hemp building—more broadly, bioconstruction—is the way these approaches bring together environmental responsibility, human well-being, and intelligent use of natural resources. Hemp is particularly fascinating because it is a fast-growing, renewable material with a very low carbon footprint, and it actually stores CO_2 as it grows. In construction, hemp-based materials offer excellent thermal and acoustic insulation, regulate humidity naturally, and create healthier indoor environments. I am inspired by the philosophy behind bioconstruction: working with nature rather than against it. It represents a shift toward more resilient, circular, and locally rooted building practices.

Daniel Daviller serves as president of Construire en Chanvre and is the technical director for eco-materials at Saint-Astier®.

What was a win for your company in the past year?

We have observed a fast-growing market (up by 20%) and have positioned ourselves internationally as a leading prefabrication supplier.

> " Hemp is particularly fascinating because it is a fast-growing, renewable material with a very low carbon footprint, and it actually stores CO_2 as it grows. "

INTERNATIONAL LISTINGS

Hempcrete Events Center at Yashu-Asa (Golden Hemp) Tochigi, Japan, built by Hiroaki Tajima of Limbs, Ltd. Construction. Photo courtesy of Ray Kaderli.

SC CAMIN DE MUR
- *Salies de Béarn*
Laurent.sainteclaque.64@gmail.com

C.G RÉNOVATION
- *Cardet*
Cg-renovation@laposte.net

SARL CHAGNOL VINCENT
- *Saint-Julien-du-Serre*
Contact: Vincent Chagnol
Chagnol.fr

CHANVRE ET BOIS
- *Saint-Romans*
Contact: Frédéric Leroy
Chanvre-et-bois.fr

MARQUES CHARPENTE
- *Le Malzieu*
Marques.charpente@orange.fr

CHARPENTERIE BOIS BRUT
- *Solliès-Pont*
Boisbrut.fr

HÉLÈNE CIARVOLA
- *Mende*
Ciaravolahelene@gmail.com

COHECO
- *Lapte*
Contact: Christophe Letang
Coheco.fr

CONSTRUCTION SAINE EN LOZÈRE
- *St Germain de Calberte*
Contact: Rémy Chorda
Contact@ecolenatio-Naleduchanvre.com

CONSTRUIRE NATURELLEMENT
- *Mignieres*
Contact: Philippe Arnaud
Construire-naturellement.fr

SARL CORREIRA MH
- *Mende*
Contact: Hugo Alves Correia
Correia-mh.fr

DB CHANVRE
- *Vidauban*
Contact: Daniel Bayol
Db-chanvre.com

DÉCORS 2 MAINS
- *Gourdon*
Decors2mains.com

JEAN-LUC DEMARES
- *Ispanac*
Malune48@gmail.com

DESTAS ET CREIB
- *Itteville*
Contact: Geoffroy Destas
Destas-et-creib.fr

DEVELGREEN
- *La Salvetat St Gilles*
Contact: Philippe Arnaud
Develgreen.fr

LES ATELIERS DE NICOLAS DRUELLE
- *Vinzieux*
Contact: Nicolas Druelle
Ateliersdruelle.fr

SCOP ECOBATI
- *St Martin de Queyriere*
Contact: Gabriel Leon
Ecobati.contact@gmail.com

ECOCENTRE DU PÉRIGORD
- *Froidefon*
Contact: Claude Micmacher
Ecocentre.org

INTERNATIONAL LISTINGS

ECO SPHERE HABITAT
- *Mundolsheim*
Contact: Sébastien Huss
Ecosphere-habitat.com

ENTERPRISE VITTE
- *Provins*
Contact: Thomas Vitte
Vittebtp.fr

E.R.C SARL - *GRAMAT*
Contact: Jean-Philippe Battut
Erc46@orange.fr

ESTRELLA RENOV' / ÉCOCHANVRE -
Saint-Gervais
Contact: Estrella Kenor
Estrella-renov.com

ETC - *Moissac*
Contact: Pierre Gatimel
Etc-batiment.fr

FB RÉNO - *Giey sur Aujon*
Fdoubou@hotmail.fr

FRANCO PORTUGAL CONSTRUCTION
- *Pegomas*
Fp-construction@orange.fr

SARL GOIMBAULT
- *Paley*
Goimbault.com

ANTOINE GUILLY
 - *Sainte-Croix*
Antoineguilly.com

LB ECOHABITAT - *Bedee*
Contact: Christophe Lubert
Lbecohabitat.fr

HABITAT ECO ACTION
- *Gabat*
Gane.entreprise@gmail.com

SCI L'HORIZON
- *Lanchaume*
Contact: Patrice Pena
Penapat09@gmail.com

ALEX KOCK
- *St Julien Chapteuil*
Alexkock@yahoo.fr

LPPDS - *Liomoors*
Lppds-platrerie@wanadoo.fr

SAS LAITHIER PÈRE ET FILS - *Uzes*
Sas.laithier@wanadoo.fr

SARL LANG
- *Saint Bardoux*
Jonathan.lang@laposte.net

MAÎTRE CUBE
- *Paris*
Contact: Jean-Philippe Estner
Maitrecube.fr

SAS MAXIME MANENC
- *Toulouse*
Maxmanenc@gmail.com

MAISON FAMILIALE RURALE DU VAL D'ERDRE - *Riaillé*
Contact: Vincent Corbard
Mfr-riaille.com

MATIERE CHANVRE
- *Nouvelle-Aquitaine*
Contact: Axel Jacqueline
Matierechanvre.com

MCP BÂTIMENT - *Paris*
Contact: Luck Valladon
Mcpbatiment.com

SARL FABIEN MICHEL
- *Saint Pierre Eynac*
Fabien.michel457@bbox.fr

Interior of hempcrete renovated 18th Century barn. Photo courtesy of IsoHemp.

INTERNATIONAL LISTINGS

Hempcrete block home. Photo courtesy of IsoHemp

MINA
- *St Germain de Calberte*
Contact: Rémy Chorda

SAS MOLLARD DELTOUR - *La Biolle*
Batisseursdepatrimoine.fr

OCTOGONE - *Nîmes*
Contact: Olivier Chambord
Bet-octogone.com

SARL LES OEUVRIERS D'ANTAN - *Marseille*
Contact: Francis Benefro
Les-oeuvriers-d-antan.fr

PALLANCHE - *Juré*
Contact: Jean Pallanche
Pallanche.fr

SARL PANELBATY
- *Beaume*
Panelbaty@hotmail.fr

PARIS HABITAT - *Paris*
Contact: Éric Pliez
Parishabitat.fr

PERSPIRANCE
- *Le Pellerin*
Contact: Arnaud Bernier
Perspirance.fr

PIEDS NUS HABITAT
- *Camjac*
Contact: Jérémie Vaissière
Piedsnushabitat.fr

PIERRE ART ET CONSTRUCTION - *Normier*
Contact: Anthony Surceaux
Pierre-art-et-construction.fr

PIERRE PAILLE CISEAUX
- *Marvejols*
Contact: Hugo Bastide
Pierrepailleciseaux@gmail.com

PIERRES CONSTRUCTION
- *Lyon*
Contact: Jean-Pierre Laurent
Pierresconstruction.com

PI-OEUVRE - *Chanu*
Contact: Anthony Stephan
Pioeuvre.fr

PIERRE QUESTIAUX
- *Tonnerre*
Pquestiaux@wanadoo.fr

SEB RENOV'ISOL
- *Mende*
Seb.renovisol@hotmail.com

INTERNATIONAL LISTINGS

RÉNOVER HABITAT - *Alès*
Contact: Frederic Allouard
Isolations-couvertures-cevennes.fr

RÉGUILLON & CIE
- *St Maurice l'Exil*
Contact: Jean-François Dubray
Reguillon.fr

ALAIN RIGAL ECORÉNOVATION CORRÈZE - *Palazingue*
Adrigal19@orange.fr

ADRIEN RISSO
- *St Remy de Provence*
Maneo16@hotmail.com

SARL S & B - *Florac*
Sbflorac.com

LAURENT SEGUIN
- *Mende*
Laurentseg48@yahoo.fr

SELE - *Mondouzil*
Contact: Christophe Sanchez
Sele.fr

SOLR ET TECHNIQUES
- *Sailly Labourse*
Contact: Olivier Vandewynckel
Solr-et-techniques.fr

SORIANO RÉNOVATION
- *Narbonne*
Contact: David Soriano
Soriano-renovation@live.fr

SOYA PEINTURE
- *Vauvert*
Contact: Yanick Vilanova
Soya.vilanova@gmail.com

STIMUL-E
- *Beaumont en Beine*
Contact: Yannick Morel
Stimul-e@orange.fr

TEMPERE CONSTRUCTION
- *Champagne sur Oise*
Contact: Kian Kamgar
Tempere-construction.fr

SARL TERRA VIVA MAÇONNERIE CASTELLANI FRÈRES - *Bastia*
Castellani-freres@gmail.com

TERRARENO - *Chambéry*
Contact: Nicolas Parent
Nicolasparent.services@gmail.com

GUILLAUME THOINET
- *Lieu dit le devet*
Thoinet.guillaume@orange.fr

TOERANA HABITAT
- *Lille*
Contact: Frédéric Cousin
Toerana-habitat.fr

TOURNÉE DU COQ
- *St. Girons*
Latourneeducoq.com

SARL LA VIE EN PIERRE
- *Les cabannes*
Contact: Clémentine Pelletier
Pelletier_clementine@orange.fr

SARL VAZ RAVALEMENT
- *Mende*
Famillevazo619@orange.fr

Hempcrete panel 81 unit building in Nantes, France with panels by Wall'up Préfa. Photo courtesy of Wall'up Préfa.

INTERNATIONAL LISTINGS

Hemp Building Materials

AGROCHANVRE
- Barenton
Hemp Hurd (Shiv) Provider
Contact: Jean-Paul Salmon
Agrochanvre-ecoconstruction.com

VIEILLE MATERIAUX (BIOSYS) - *Étalans*
Hemp Blocks
Contact: Cédric Gervais
Vieille-materiaux.com

AGNA - *Clermont-Ferrand*
Insulation Batts, Acoustic Batts
Contact: Nicolas Lounis
Acoustique-agna.fr

BCB BIOSOURCÉS ET CHAUX BUSINESS
- Chatillon le Duc
Hemp Building Materials Supplier; Hemp Hurd (Shiv) Provider; Lime/binder Provider
Contact: Jean Marc Pellen

CAVAC
- La Roche-sur-Yon Cedex
Hemp Hurd (Shiv) Provider; Insulation Batts
Contact: Olivier Joreau
Cavac-biomateriaux.com

LA CHANVRIÈRE
- Saint Lye
Hemp Hurd (Shiv) Provider
Contact: Marie Laure Moreau
Lachanvriere.com

WALLUP PREFA - *Aulnoy*
Drywall; Hemp Panels
Contact: Philippe Lamarque
Wallup.fr

Equipment Sales Rental

Featured
QUADRA CONCRETE
- Contamine-sur-Arve
Block Robotics
40, route de Findrol
74130 Contamines-sur-Arve
Contact: Xavier Delacour
(+33) 4.50.03.92.21
Info@quadra-concrete.com
Quadra-concrete.com

AKTA BVP - *Baud*
Contact: Laurent Goudet
Akta-bvp.fr

EREASY (BAUMER CHANVRE)
- Saint-Vit
Contact: Damien Baumer
Baumer-ereasy.business.site

Financial Services

AUGUR ASSOCIATES
- Paris
Contact: Christophe Nourissier
Augur.associates

Lime Binder Supplier

BAO FORMATION
- Marseille
Contact: Laurent Tainturier
Baoformation.fr

C-E-S-A (SAINT ASTIER)
- Saint Astier
Contact: Daniel Daviller
C-e-s-a.fr

GROUPE VICAT SA
- Paris La Défense Cedex
Contact: Marco Cappellari
Vicat.com

SAINT-GOBAIN-WEBER
- Sucy-en-Brie, Île-de-France
Contact: Jean Marc Allorent
Saint-gobain.com/en/weber

SOCLI - *Yzaourt*
Contact: Pierre-Alexandre LePlante
Socli.fr

Hempcrete Town Hall in Trello Netherlands. Photo courtesy of Dermot Moore.

LEADER PROFILE
SUSANNE BARTHOLOMÉ
A Sustainable Hemp Value Chain can offer a Real Alternative to Coal in Regions Undergoing Structural Change

I am the leader of a junior research group focusing on bio-based raw materials (hemp). Our interdisciplinary team investigates how the hemp value chain needs to be structured to be sustainable and provide an alternative to coal in the Lake Geiseltal structural change region.

I am particularly drawn to the concept of nature-connected building. Hemp construction enables the tangible integration of natural materials and living spaces, where materiality, structure and indoor climate work together to create buildings that are technically robust and deeply connected to their natural surroundings. To me, this represents a genuine engineering approach to integrating nature and housing, rather than a purely symbolic or decorative gesture.

What was a win for your company in the past year?

In addition to my role at Merseburg University of Applied Sciences, I am the Chairwoman of the Hanffaser Geiseltal cooperative. We were founded in 2022 and already purchased the land and buildings in 2023, where we are building a fibre processing plant for hemp straw.

What is something about hemp building/construction/processing you didn't know a year ago?

Over the past few months, I have learned a great deal about the various stages involved in spraying with hemp-lime. It is amazing how simple yet effective this process is. This process is also now being adapted for use with clay and hemp, which will be advantageous for our regional building materials value chain, given the abundance of clay deposits in the area.

Dr.-Ing Susanne Bartholomé, is CEO of Hanffaser Geiseltal and researcher at Merseburg University of Applied Sciences.

> *" It's a genuine engineering approach to integrating nature and housing, rather than a purely symbolic or decorative gesture. "*

INTERNATIONAL LISTINGS

GERMANY

EUROPEAN INDUSTRIAL HEMP ASSOCIATION
- *Wolfsburg*
Contact: Daniel Kruse
Eiha.org

ABW SHOP - *Berlin*
Hemp Hurd (Shiv) Provider; Lime/binder Provider; Training Provider
Contact: Sven Hänichen
Abwshop.de

DURAHEMP GMBH
- *Berlin*
Architect, Hemp Blocks
Contact: Gökcan Güney
Durahemp.de

WILHELM G CLASEN GMBH - *Hamburg*
Natural Fibers
Contact: Peter Clausen
Clausen@WGC.de

ROGER DAUER - *Berlin*
Architect
Rogerdauer@posteo.net

HANF UND KALK - *Legau*
Green Builder; Hempcrete Installer; Training Provider; Plaster
Contact: Reinhold Straub
Hanfundkalk.de

HANFBAUKOLLEKTIV
- *Berlin, Leipzig*
Engineer; Educational Institution; Training Provider
Contact: Roman Schultz, Felix Drewes
Hanfbaukollektiv.com

HANFINGENIEUR - *Berlin*
Engineer; Green Builder; Hemp Hurd (Shiv) Provider; Hempcrete Installer
Contact: Henrik Pauly
Hanfingenieur.de

ROMAN KALK - *Wangeling*
Lime/binder Provider; Plaster
Contact: Norbert Höpfer
Romankalk.webs.com

SMARTER HABITAT GMBH & CO. KG - *Munich*
Fiberboard
Contact: Datty Ruth
Smarter-habitat.com

THERMO-HANF
- *Nördlingen*
Hemp Batt Insulation; Hemp Panels
Contact: Ulla Schrödersecker
Thermo-hanf.de/en/

VON HANF (HEMPLITH)
- *Hohenaspe*
Green Builder; Hempcrete Installer; Drywall; Fiberboard; Insulation Batts; Hemp Blocks
Contact: Tim Lange
Vonhanf.de

HUNGARY

KENDER BETON HAZ
Green Builder; Hempcrete Installer
Kenderbetonhaz.hu

MONIC TREND KFT.
- *Ócsa*
Green Builder; Hempcrete Installer
Contact: Béla Horesnyi
Monictrend.hu

Hempcrete home built in northern Germany. Photo courtesy of Tim Lange.

LEADER PROFILE
GÖKCAN GÜNEY/ROGER DAUER
Hempcrete is a Rare Combination of Low-Tech inputs and High-Tech Performance.

At DuraHemp, we are building Germany's first regional production facility on an industrial level for prefabricated hempcrete elements, with an initial focus on blocks. Roger leads product development as well as certification and approval processes, while I concentrate on optimizing production workflows so hemp-based building materials can be manufactured consistently and adopted more easily by the local construction industry.

Hemp fascinates me because of its incredible versatility and regenerative potential. I often call it "soul food for soil." It creates value at every level of the supply chain—regenerating land, offering viable economics for farmers, and delivering high-performance, sustainable products for consumers. What excites me most is that hemp-based materials can compete with conventional construction products while using resources far more efficiently.

In construction, hempcrete represents a rare combination of low-tech inputs and high-tech performance. Producing hempcrete products in consistent high-quality is not simple, but that complexity is what motivates us. The technical challenges make the work both demanding and deeply rewarding.

Over the past year, I've learned how critical hemp hurd quality is—especially particle size distribution and dust content—when producing prefabricated elements. While in-situ applications allow for adjustment, serial and automated production demand precise and consistent raw materials.

Looking ahead, one of the biggest challenges is building reliable regional value chains. By working with industrial partners and universities to define clear specifications and standards, we aim to support farmers, stabilize quality, and make hemp construction a dependable option for builders and architects.

Roger Dauer (L) & Gökcan Güney (R) are co-founders of DuraHemp, based in Berlin, Germany.

INTERNATIONAL LISTINGS

ICELAND

LUDIKA - *Reykjavík*
Architect
Contact: Anna Karlsdóttir
Ludika.is

INDIA

GREENJAMS
- *Roorkee, Uttarakhand*
Hemp Blocks; Green Builder; Engineer
Contact: Tarun Jami
Greenjams.org

GOHEMP AGROVENTURES - *Uttarakhand*
Architect, Green Builder, Hempcrete Installer
Contact: Gaurav Dixit
Gohemp.in

HEMP SLAP ECO-CONSTRUCTION
- *Uttarakhand*
Contact: Haneesh Katnawer
Himalayanhemp.in

NAMRATA HEMPCO LIMITED - *Bangalore*
Equipment Sales/Rental
Contact: Namrata Kandwal
Nhempco.com

INDONESIA

ALTARIZE - *Bali*
Plasters, Hempcrete Installation
Contact: Edgar Concepcion
Altarize.com

IRELAND

INTERNATIONAL HEMP BUILDING ASSN.
- *County Kerry*
Hemp Consulting
Contact: Steve Allin
Internationalhempbuilding.org

GRÁHEMP - *Limerick*
Hemp Blocks, Hemp Wool Insulation, Hemp/Lime Plasters, and Lime Renders
Contact: Jason Quille
Grahemp.ie

HEMP BUILD SUSTAINABLE PRODUCTS LTD.
- *Leinster*
Green Builder, Hemp Building Materials Supplier, Hempcrete Installer, Training Provider
Hempbuild.ie

HEMPBUILD
- *County Meath*
Hemp Hurd (Shiv) Provider; Lime/binder Provider; Green Builder; Hemp Blocks
Contact: Shane McDermott

TRADITIONAL LIME COMPANY
- *County Carlow*
Hemp Hurd (Shiv) Provider; Lime/Binder Provider
Contact: Edward Byrne
Traditionallime.ie

ISRAEL

TAV GROUP - *Haifa*
Architects
Contact: Maoz Alon
Tavgroup.com

NETIV7 - *Tel Aviv*
Lime/binder Provider
Contact: Norbert Hoepfer
Sites.google.com/site/netiv7/Home

Hemp-insulated warehouse space in Sweden. Photo courtesy of Ekolution.

INTERNATIONAL LISTINGS

ITALY

EQUILIBRIUM SRL
Educational Institution; Engineer; Green Builder; Hempcrete Installer; Training Provider
Contact: Gilberto Barcella
Equilibrium-bioedilizia.com

SENINI - *Novagli di Montichiari*
Hemp Blocks
Contact: Michele Pavoni
Senini.it

SCHÖNTHALER OHG - *Eyrs*
Hemp Blocks
Contact: Werner Schönthaler
Hanfstein.eu

SOUTH HEMP TECNO SRL - *Crispiano/Taranto*
Hemp Hurd (Shiv) Provider
Contact: Rachele Invernizzi
Southemp.com

JAPAN

LIMBS LIMITED CONSTRUCTION -*Tochigi*
Contact: Hiroaki "Mahuru" Tajima
Tajima@limbs.co.jp

LATVIA

INBOKSS SIA
Hemp Processing Equipment
Contact: Kristaps Eglitas
Hurdmaster.com

NATURENEST
- *Ikšķile, Ogre region*
Hempcrete Installer; Lime/binder Provider, Hemp Hurd (Shiv) Provider
Contact: Ugis Paurins
Naturenest.lv

OBELISK FARM
- *Obeliškas*
Training Provider
Contact: Andris Visnevskis
Obeliskfarm.lv

LITHUANIA

UAB NATURAL FIBER
- *Vilnius*
Hemp Processor; Hemp Hurd (Shiv) Provider
Contact: Liucija Samuolytė
Naturalfiber.eu

HEMPBALT - *Kaunas*
Green Builder; Hempcrete Installer; Lime/binder Provider
Contact: Juozas Jankauskas
Hempbalt.com

MEXICO

A10STUDIO - *Cabo*
Architect
Contact: Mariano Arias-Diez
A10Studio.net

HEAVENGROWN
- *Tulum*
Green Builder; Hemp Processor; Hempcrete Installer; Hemp Blocks
Contact: Stephen Clarke
Heavengrown.com

MICROPOZ - *Morelos*
Lime/binder Provider
Contact: Samuel Alanís
Micropoz.com

Hempcrete and bamboo ecotourism treehouse, Tulum, Mexico. Photo courtesy of Heaven Grown.

HEMP BUILDING DIRECTORY 2026

LEADER PROFILE

GAURAV DIXIT
Hemp is Scalable in Industrial and Rural Economies

GoHemp's mission is to build 1,000 hemp buildings by 2030 and make India a global leader in green construction using hemp.

The idea of "green" buildings comes from plants—so why not actually use plants in buildings? Hemp is one of the most versatile plants, scalable both industrially and at decentralized rural levels. It connects agriculture with construction, reduces carbon emissions, lowers building energy use, and decreases dependence on non-renewable resources.

Gaurav Dixit is co-founder of GoHemp, based in New Delhi, India.

end-to-end hemp construction company.

I formerly saw hemp as a premium material. This year, my focus shifted to making hemp affordable. If hemp stays premium, it won't scale—mainstream adoption needs cost-effective solutions.

Key challenges include policy gaps, uneven state regulations, lack of processing infrastructure and machinery, low awareness, and absence from building codes and tender specifications. These will be solved through policy clarity, ecosystem development, and industry collaboration.

What was a win for your company in the past year?

In the last year, we trained over 150 people, contributed to four hemp-based projects, processed more than 100 tons of hemp, and worked with around 150 women farmers. We are building GoHemp as an

> " *The idea of 'green' buildings comes from plants—so why not actually use plants in buildings?* "

INTERNATIONAL LISTINGS

Hemp house in Ommen, Netherlands. Courtesy Dun Agro Hemp Group.

NEPAL

SHAH HEMP INNOVENTURES - *Kathmandu*
Green Builder; Hemp Hurd (Shiv) Provider; Hempcrete Installer; Lime/binder Provider
Contact: Dhiraj Shah
Shahhempinnoventures.com

NETHERLANDS

Association

BIOMIMICRY NL - *Utrecht*
Contact: Saskia van den Muijsenberg
Biomimicrynl.org

KALKHENNEP NEDERLAND - *Houten*
Kalkhennepnederland.nl

STROBOUW NEDERLAND - *Nijverdal*
Contact: Emmanuel Laugs
Vakgroepstrobouw.org

VIBA - *Zeist*
Contact: Joop Bensdorp
Vibavereniging.nl

Architect/Designer

PLATFORM3 - *Houten*
Contact: Ralf van Tongeren
Duurzame-architect.com

ORIO ARCHITECTEN - *Soest*
Contact: Michel Post
Orioarchitecten.nl

ARCHITECTENLAB - *Deventer*
Contact: Marc Harmsen
Architectenlab.nl

OZ ARCHITECT - *Amsterdam*
Contact: Oresti Sarafopoulos
Ozarchitect.nl

WERKSTATT - *Eindhoven*
Contact: Niels Groeneveld
Werkstatt.nu

Green Builder/Hempcrete Installer

DUN AGRO - *Oude Pekela*
Green Builder; Hemp Building Materials Supplier; Engineer; Hempcrete Installer; Researcher/Developer; Architect; Hemp Panels; Hemp Blocks
Contact: Albert Dun
Dunagro.nl

ECOBOUWSALLAND - *Heino*
Contact: Rens Borgers
Ecobouwsalland.nl

G.D.H. BOUW BV - *Weesp*
Contact: Gijs den Hartog
Gdhbouw.nl

WANDSTYLING - *Burgh Haamstede*
Contact: Erik Jonkers
Wandstyling.com

INTERNATIONAL LISTINGS

Hemp Building Materials

HEMPFLAX
- *Oude Pekela*
Hemp Building Materials Supplier; Fiberboard; Insulation Batts; Hemp Blocks
Contact: Mark Reinders
Hempflax.com

ROOZEN & ROOZEN
- *Zundert*
Contact: Johan Roozen
Roozenenroozen.nl

NEW ZEALAND

HEMP BUILDING ASSOCIATION NEW ZEALAND
Hba.nz

OZHEMP NEW ZEALAND
Hemp Hurd (Shiv) Provider, Lime Binder Provider
Contact: Donald Khoo
Ozhemp.com.au

RUBISCO - *Christchurch*
Hemp Processor; Hemp Hurd (Shiv) Provider
Contact: Craig Carr
Rubisco.co.nz

Architect:

BLACK PINE ARCHITECTS
Architect
Contact: Duncan Sinclair
Blackpine.co.nz

KEIRON O'CONNELL ARCHITECTURE
- *Invercargill*
Contact: Keiron O'Connell
Koarchitecture.co.nz

ULENBERG ECO-ARCHITECTS LIMITED - *Auckland*
Contact: Martin Ulenberg
Ulenberg.co.nz

Green Builder/ Hempcrete Installer

ERKHART CONSTRUCTION
- *Wanaka*
Contact: Locky Urquhart
Erkhartconstruction.co.nz

KOHU HEMP - *Takaka*
Contact: Antoine Tane
Kohuhemp.nz

ROCKSTEAD CONSTRUCTION/ GEOBIND - *Kerikeri*
Contact: Doug Sturrock
rocksteadconstruction.co.nz/
Geobind.co.nz

Hempcrete cabin in Slovenia by CoGreen Konopljine. Photo courrtesy of Primož Zorec.

INTERNATIONAL LISTINGS

POLAND

Featured
HEMPIRE INTERNATIONAL
Pl. Jana Kilińskiego 2, 35-005 Rzeszów
Green Builder; Engineer; Architect; Hempcrete Installer; Hemp (Shiv) Provider; Hemp Lime Binder Provider
Contact: Sergiy Kovalenkov
(380) 67 658 5350
Hempire.Tech

INSTITUTE OF NATURAL FIBRES AND MEDICINAL PLANTS - *Poznan*
Educational Institution; Hemp Processor; Hemp Hurd (Shiv) Provider
Contact: Gregory Spycnalski, Witold Czeszak
Iwnirz.pl

Architect/Designer:

OGÓLNOPOLSKIE STOWARZYSZENIE BUDOWNICTWA NATURALNEGO (OSBN)
- *Warszawa*
Contact: Maciej Jagielak, Tomasz Zmyślony
Osbn.pl

TOMASZ MIELCZYŃSKI
- *Czarnków*
Architect
Txma.pl

WIOSKA KONOPNA
Architect; Green Builder; Training Provider
Contact: Maciej Pawłowski
Wioskakonopna.pl

ARCHITEKT PAWEL WOLEJSZA - *Warsaw*
Architect, Engineer
Pawel.wolejsza@gmail.com

Green Builder/ Hempcrete Installer/ Supplier

BETONIKA - *Grodziczno*
Contact: Kornelia Rozwadowska
Betonika-dev.webflow.io

BUDYNKI Z KONOPI
- *Świdnik*
Contact: Przemysław Brzyski
Budynkizkonopi.pl

COSTKA - *Suwałki*
Contact: Marcin Kacprzyk
Costka.com

DOMIR - *Poznan*
Contact: Paweł Fornalski
Domir.com.pl/en

PRACOWNIA ZIELONY ŁOSKOT
- *Tychy*
Contact: Artur Łoskot
Zielonyloskot.pl

FOLNY HEMP
-*Wierzchosławice*
Contact: Lukasz Knapik
Folnyhemp.pl

GREEN LANES - *Lublin*
Contact: Piotrek Pietras
Greenlanes.pl

HEMP SYSTEM
Contact: Mikołaj Wojciechowski
Hempsystem.pl

HEMPFY BLOCKS
- *Olsztyn*
Contact: Wojciech Wiechnik
Hempfyblock.com

PODLASKIE KONOPIE
Contact: Piotr Jastrzębski
Podlaskiekonopie.pl

SANTERRA NATURAL BUILDERS - *Rzeszów*
Contact: Łukasz Jaworski
Zdrowetynki.pl

STRUKTURE POLSKA
Contact: Max Germain
Strukturepolska@gmail.com

UNIBUILD - *Gorzów Wlkp.*
Unibuild.pl

Portuguese 14th Century water mill renovated by Natura Matéria. Photo by Carlos Cardos.

INTERNATIONAL LISTINGS

PORTUGAL

CANHAMORHEMP
- *Colos*
Hemp Blocks
Contact: Elad Kaspin
Canhamorhemp.com

NATURA MATÉRIA
- *Guimarães*
Hemp Blocks; Hemp hurd(Shiv); Lime Binder
Contact: César Cardoso
Naturamateria.pt

TERRAVIVA - *Aljezur, Faro*
Contact: Andrea Abad
Terraviva.pt

VIMAPLÁS - *Canelas*
Contact: Ricardo Couto
Vimaplas.pt

SAUDI ARABIA

GREEN DESERT - *Riyadh*
Hemp Blocks; Hemp hurd(Shiv)
Contact: Abdulhadi "Hadi" Al-Amer
Greendesert.sa

SERBIA

LJUBICA ARSIĆ - *Belgrade*
Architect
Ljubicaarsic.com

HEMPLICITY - *Belgrade*
Green Builder; Hempcrete Installer; Architect
Contact: Predrag Milosavljević
Hemplicity.co

SLOVAKIA

ZEM DESIGN
Architect; Engineer; Green Builder
Contact: Michael Rice
Zem.design

SLOVENIA

COGREEN - *Ljubljana*
Engineer; Green Builder; Hempcrete Installer; Insulation Batts; Fiberboard
Contact: Primoz Zorec
Cogreen.si

SOUTH AFRICA

AFRIMAT HEMP
- *Capetown*
Hemp Blocks
Contact: Boshoff Muller
Afrimathemp.co.za

HEMPORIUM SA
- *Constantia*
Educational Institution; Hemp Building Materials Supplier; Green Builder; Researcher/Developer
Contact: Tony Budden
Hemporium.com

WOLF & WOLF ARCHITECTS
- *Capetown*
Architect
Contact: Wolf
Wolfandwolf.co.za

Hempcrete Home in Serbia with goats, built by Hemplicity. Photo courtesy Sonja Lazukic

INTERNATIONAL LISTINGS

SPAIN

BESTBLOCK - *Almería*
Hemp Blocks
Contact: Alberto Viciana
Bestblock.ibo.company

CANNATEKTUM (CANNABRIC)
- *Granada*
Green Builder; Engineer; Architect; Training Provider; Hemp Blocks; Plaster
Contact: Monica Brümmer
Cannabric.com

HEMPCRETE SPAIN
- *Castellón*
Hemp Blocks
Contact: Raquel Sanchis
Hempcrete.es

IBERCANEM - *Girona*
Hemp Processor
Contact: Esau Rodriguez
Ibercanem.com

SWEDEN

DALARO HAMPA & MILJO AB - *Stockholm*
Hemp Hurd (Shiv) Provider; Hempcrete Installer; Fiberboard; Drywall; Insulation Batts
Contact: Mari Elfving
Hampvaruhuset.se

EKOLUTION AB - *Malmö*
Insulation batts
Contact: Remi Loren
Ekolution.se

RE:ECO SOLUTIONS
Reecosolutions.se

SWITZERLAND

ARBIO SA - *Vaud*
Green Builder
Contact: Pascal Favre
Arbio.ch

BAUMSCHLAGER EBERLE ARCHITEKTEN
- *Gallen*
Architect
Contact: Tanja Sprünken
Baumschlager-eberle.com/en/

JOOST VERSTRAETE
- *Geneva*
Architect

RETHINK MATERIALS KOLLEKTIV HEMP ECO SYSTEMS GROUP
- *Oberkirch*
Architect; Engineer; Green Builder; Hemp (Shiv) Supplier; Lime/binder Provider
Contact: Hans Peter Hviid
Hempecosystems.org

HANFKALK BAU
- *Oberkirch*
Green Builder
Contact: Toni Läderach
Hempecosystems.org/hanFkalkbau-ch

HOTZ PARTNER - *Zurich*
Architect, Green Builder
Contact: Daniel Vega
Hotzpartner.ch

OPENLY - *Altstätten*
Green Builder, Carbon Credits
Contact: Andy Keel
Openly.systems

SCHÖB AG - *Gams*
Green Builder
Contact: Philipp Schöb
Schoeb-ag.ch

THAILAND

ALTARIZE THAILAND
- *Chiang Mai*
Plasters, hempcrete installation
Contact: Edgar Concepcion
Altarize.com

Swiss hempcrete home renovation. Photo courtesy of Werner Schönthaler

INTERNATIONAL LISTINGS

UKRAINE

Featured
HEMPIRE INTERNATIONAL - *Kyiv*
Hempire.Tech
Green Builder; Engineer; Architect; Hempcrete Installer; Hemp (Shiv) Provider; Hemp Lime Binder Provider
Contact: Sergiy Kovalenkov
(380) 67 658 5350

K.TEX LLC - *Irpin*
Hemp (Shiv) Provider
Contact: Viacheslav (Slava) Voitko
Ktex.ua

UNITED KINGDOM

Architect/Engineer

BAILLIE BAILLIE ARCHITECTS
- *Glasgow, Scotland*
Contact: Colin Baillie
Baillie-baillie.co.uk

CAIRN ARCHITECTS - *London*
Contact: Kieran Hawkins
Cairnarchitects.com

COMMONBOND ARCHITECTS - *London*
Contact: Graham Mateer
Commonbond.studio

CHRIS DAVIES ARCHITECT
- *Gloucestershire*
Architect
Chrisdaviesarchitect.co.uk

ECOLOGICAL ARCHITECTURE - *Aberfeldy*
Architect
Contact: Sue Manning
Ecological-architecture.co.uk

JSA ARCHITECTS - *Derby*
Architect
Contact: Justin Smith
Jsa.design

GLENN HOWELLS ARCHITECTS - *London*
Architect, Engineer
Glennhowells.co.uk

MARK HINES - *London*
Architect
Markhines.co.uk

INVISIBLE STUDIO
- *Chippenham*
Contact: Piers Taylor
Invisiblestudio.org

MATERIAL CULTURES
- *London*
Architect, Green Builder
Contact: Paloma Gormley
Materialcultures.org

MIKHAIL RICHES
- *London*
Architect
Mikhailriches.com

MODECE ARCHITECTS
- *Stowmarket*
Architect
Contact: Matt Bell
Modece.com

CLARE NASH ARCHITECTURE - *Banbury*
Architect
Contact: Clare Nash
Clarenasharchitecture.co.uk

Hempcrete waterside home in Scottish Highlands designed by Roderick James Architects. Photo courtesy of Kim Sayer.

LEADER PROFILE
RAQUEL SANCHIS ULACIA
Bioconstruction Brings Material Behaviour, Climate, and Human Health into the Center of Architectural Thinking

We distribute hemp-lime construction systems, but just as importantly, we support architects and builders in understanding how to design and build with them properly. A big part of my role is translating technical knowledge into practical decisions on real projects, while also working to strengthen the wider hemp construction ecosystem in Spain.

Bioconstruction brings material behaviour, climate, and human health back into the center of architectural thinking. Modern construction often focuses almost exclusively on airtightness and insulation values, without properly considering how walls actually manage moisture and air over time. In a Mediterranean climate, this is a fundamental issue. Hemp-lime works with vapor permeability, thermal inertia, and moisture buffering in a way that makes buildings more resilient, more comfortable, and ultimately more durable.

Raquel Sanchis Ulacia is founder and director of Hempcrete Spain, located in Castellón

What was a win for your company in the past year?

A real win this year was seeing a shift in how people approach us. We are increasingly contacted not just as a supplier, but as a technical partner. In addition, we participated in the first public building project in Spain constructed with hemp, which marked an important milestone for the material's acceptance at an institutional level.

What is something about hemp building/construction/processing you didn't know a year ago?

This year I learned how much resistance to change still comes from habit rather than evidence. Once professionals see the material in practice, understand the physics behind it, and work with it hands-on, skepticism often disappears.

> " *Hemp-lime works with vapor permeability, thermal inertia, and moisture buffering to create more resilient buildings.* "

INTERNATIONAL LISTINGS

Hempcrete 'Renewable House' at Building Research Establishment (BRE) Innovation Park in Watford, England. Photo courtesy of Linford Group.

NATIVE ARCHITECTS
- *York*
Architect; Green Builder
Contact: Sally Kirk Walker
Nativearchitects.com

NOEL WRIGHT ARCHITECTS
- *Hampshire*
Architect
Noelwrightarchitects.co.uk

PRACTICE ARCHITECTURE - *London*
Architect
Contact: David Grandorge
Practicearchitecture.co.uk

REED WATTS ARCHITECTS - *London*
Contact: Jim Reed
Reedwatts.com

SKIDMORE, OWINGS & MERRILL - *London*
Architect; Engineer
Contact: Kent Jackson
Som.com

TIMOTHY TASKER ARCHITECTS - *London*
Contact: Timothy Tasker
Ttarchitects.co.uk

TUCKEY DESIGN STUDIO - *London*
Contact: Jonathan Tuckey
Tuckeydesign.com

VINCENT-GORBING
- *Hertfordshire*
Architect
Contact: Stephen Chown
Vincent-gorbing.co.uk
GreenBuilder/Hempcrete Installer

ECO RENOVATION-UK
- *London*
Contact: Adam Illes
Eco-renovation.co.uk

EAST YORKSHIRE HEMP
- *Brandesburton*
Contact: Nick Voase
Eastyorkshirehemp.co.uk

GREENCORE HOMES
- *Oxfordshire*
Contact: Ian Pritchett
Greencoreconstruction.co.uk

HAMMOND HEMP HOMES - *Warrington*
Contact: Carl Hemmond
Hammondhemphomes.co.uk

HEMSPAN - *Cambridge*
Contact: Matthew Belcher
Hemspan.com

HEMP CONSTRUCTION
- *Standerwick, Frome*
Contact: Ryn Luxmore
Hempconstruction.co.uk

HEMP-LIME SPRAY LTD.
- *Wymondham*
Contact: Graham Durrant
Hemplimespray.co.uk

HINDS BUILDING SERVICES - *Darlington*
Contact: Omawale Oginga Hinds
Hindsbuilding.co.uk

HEMP BUILDING DIRECTORY 2026

LEADER PROFILE

IAN PRITCHETT
10,000 UK Hempcrete Homes by 2035

The UK's Greencore Homes, one of the largest hemp-lime builders in the country, announced two large British housing development projects in 2026 featuring the company's "Biond panels" totaling more than 130 new "Better Than Net Zero" homes in Oxfordshire and Buckinghamshire. The UK government's Homes England will provide £8 million to "turbocharge housebuilding for small and medium-sized enterprise (SME) builders," the company said.

Co-founder and Innovation Director Ian Pritchett's foray into sustainable building began in the early 2000s, driven by a desire to reintroduce traditional materials into new construction in the so-called "Lime Revival" movement in Britain.

This success led Pritchett to explore other environmentally friendly applications for lime, eventually leading him to hemp. He credits architect Ralph Carpenter in Suffolk, UK, (considered to be the "grandfather of UK hempcrete") as a pioneer in using hemp and lime, having learned from French techniques. "I was impressed with what Ralph was doing," Pritchett said. The company also worked for about 12 years with building science researchers and engineers at the University of Bath to nail down the properties of hemp-lime that would work best in the UK. Pritchett made the pivotal decision to sell his historic building business and focus entirely on new builds, especially with lime and hemp. "That's what I've been doing for the last twenty years," he said.

Ian Pritchett, co-founder and innovation director of Greencore Homes, IN.Courtesy of Greencore Homes

Early on, Greencore steadily built houses and non-domestic buildings, completing 150 to 200 houses and about 50 non-domestic buildings over five years, Pritchett said. The pandemic slowed them down, but so did the wet-mix, on-site application of hemp and lime, particularly during inclement weather. A harsh winter in 2010, where 85 houses were being cast simultaneously, caused significant delays. Bad weather and a wet mix meant the company incurred a substantial weekly penalty on a project for Marks and Spencer's at Cheshire Oaks.

"That focused our minds," Pritchett recalled. This experience led the company to adopt a panelized system. "We would make the panels in a factory, cast the lime of hemp into them, and we would dry it in the factory as well. And that was probably the best decision we ever made."

Fifteen years ago, a panel would take six weeks to make and dry; now, the process takes only 24 to 48 hours.

Greencore's "Biond panels" feature a 120-millimeter (five-inch) layer of hempcrete combined with seven inches of wood fiber insulation, resulting in a 12-inch thick panel. "Overall, you've got a panel that's 12 inches thick," Pritchett explained. The company's factory currently has the capacity to produce 200 houses a year, with plans to scale up to that rate by early 2026.

Pritchett emphasized the benefits of combining hempcrete with Passive House principles. While hempcrete is a good insulator, he noted it's not the "best insulation material" on its own for achieving Passive House standards without extremely thick walls. The company's composite biopanel, with both hempcrete and wood fiber, addresses this by improving thermal performance and significantly reducing drying times. "If you bring the two things together, you get the best of both worlds," Pritchett said. Other Passive House methodologies Greencore uses are optimal house orientation for solar gain; minimizing surface area to reduce heat loss and sufficient shading to prevent overheating in summer.

Each Greencore home has a 262 kWp roof-integrated solar PV system. Coupled with good insulation, airtightness, and mechanical ventilation with heat recovery, these elements contribute to "a fantastic house."

All in all, Pritchett's journey from historic preservation to leading a modern hemp-lime construction company has been a pragmatic approach to sustainable building. He noted that the UK has no regulations about embodied carbon in housing and no subsidies for hemp building.

"Everything we've done has had to stack up commercially," he said.

Greencore Homes works with the British government to build high-performing "Better than Zero" Passive House homes with hemp panels. Image courtesy Greencore Homes

INTERNATIONAL LISTINGS

HUMAN NATURE
- Lewes
Contact: Jonathan Smales
Humannature-places.com

STANWIX LTD
- Buckinghamshire
Contact: Will Stanwix
Thathempcreteguy.com

UK HEMPCRETE
- Chesterfield
Contact: Alex Sparrow
UKHempcrete.com

WELSTEAD HOME
- Devon
Contact: Rory Watson
Welsteadhome.com

Hemp Building Materials Supply

ALLIANCE FOR SUSTAINABLE BUILDING PRODUCTS *- London*
Contact: Simon Corbey
Asbp.org.uk

ADAPTAVATE LTD.
- Berkshire
Fiberboard; Plaster; Other Hemp materials
Contact: Tom Robinson
Adaptavate.com

BIOTWIN *- London*
Hemp composite studs
Contact: Kit Chong
Biotwin.co.uk

ERTHLY *- Hampshire*
Hemp Composites
Contact: Riff Hutchinson
Erthly.co.uk

FARM ED *- Oxfordshire*
Contact: Ian Wilkinson
Farm-ed.co.uk

GRWNGROUP *- London*
Batt insulation
Contact: Nick Joyce
Grwngroup.com

HG MATTHEWS
- Buckinghamshire
Hemp Blocks
Contact: Will Matthews
Hgmatthews.com

Oaklee Housing Assn. hempcrete social housing scheme buildings in Northern Ireland. Photo courtesy The Last Straw.

INTERNATIONAL LISTINGS

Restored hemp home in East Yorkshire by Nick Voase. Photo courtesy of Lillian Clarke.

HEMP BLOCK COMPANY - *Chesham*
Hemp Blocks; Hemp Panels
Contact: Neil Stephen
Hempblock.co.uk

INDINATURE
- *Scottish Borders*
Insulation Batts
Contact: Scott Simpson
Indinature.co

NATURAL BUILDING STORE - *Matlock*
Contact: Alex Sparrow
Naturalbuildingstore.com

NATURAL BUILDING SYSTEMS AND MATERIALS RESEARCH, LTD
- *Palgrave*
Hemp Blocks, Hemp Panels
Contact: Chloe Donovan
Naturalbuildingsystems.com

Lime Binder Supplier

ANGLIA LIME COMPANY
Contact: Graham Griffiths
Anglialime.com

CORNISH LIME COMPANY
Cornishlime.co.uk

LIME GREEN PRODUCTS, LTD.
- *Shropshire*
Contact: Dominic Putnam
Limegreeen.co.uk

OXHORN LIMEWORKS
- *Sheffield*
Contact: Rogan Parkin
Oxhornlimeworks.co.u

ST. ASTIER UK
Contact: Ranson Og
Stastier.co.uk

UNITY LIME
- *Worminghall*
Contact: James David King
Unitylime.co.uk

WALES

HEMPCRETE CYMRU
Green Builder; Hempcrete Installer
Contact: Ronan & Jasper
Hempcretecymru.com

TY-MAWR LIME LTD
- *Brecon*
Contact: Joyce Gervis
Lime.org.uk

WELLSPRING HOMES
- *Cardiff*
Green builder, hempcrete installer
Contact: Hadleigh Hobbs
Wellspringhomes-co.uk

www.ingramcontent.com/pod-product-compliance
Lightning Source LLC
Chambersburg PA
CBHW060502030426
42337CB00015B/1692